Made for Love

MADE FOR LOVE

Same-Sex Attractions
and the Catholic Church

Father Michael Schmitz

Ignatius Press–Augustine Institute

San Francisco   Greenwood Village, CO

Ignatius Press Distribution
1915 Aster Rd
Sycamore, IL 60178
Tel: (800) 651-1531
www.ignatius.com

Augustine Institute
6160 S. Syracuse Way, Suite 310
Greenwood Village, CO 80111
Tel: (866) 767-3155
www.augustineinstitute.org

Cover Design: Ben Dybas

Reprinted 2021.
© 2017 by Ignatius Press, San Francisco,
and the Augustine Institute, Greenwood Village, CO
All rights reserved.
ISBN 978-1-62164-219-0 (PB)
ISBN 978-1-68149-795-2 (eBook)
Library of Congress Control Number: 2017948977

Printed in Canada ∞

Contents

Foreword   vii

Introduction   xi

1. At the Beginning   1

2. What-It-Is-Ness   13

3. Search Your Feelings....
    You Know It to Be True   27

4. The T-Word   37

5. Good but Fallen   47

6. Made for Love   55

7. Identity   73

8. What Are You Looking For?   85

9. Same-Sex Attractions in the Church   99

10. Dealing with Definitions   115

11. Where Is That in the Bible?   127

12. A Real Relationship   141

13. Questions and Answers   155

14. The Ultimate Question   169

Foreword

"O Lord, who are you? O Lord, who am I?" This simple, profound prayer seems tailor-made for young people at the beginning of the twenty-first century. We're caught up like never before in a quest to define ourselves, to understand what makes us who we are, what's going to make someone notice and care about us. The fact that this prayer was uttered at the beginning of the *thirteenth* century, by the young Saint Francis of Assisi, reminds us that this human longing is a universal experience. But it's also a challenge: it asks the question in a way that is not often appreciated today.

"Who am I?" is an important question, but we often ask the wrong audience. The answer won't be found on the Internet. It can't be crowdsourced, or found in an online poll, or measured in likes or shares or retweets. But it seems like the more connected social media becomes, the more disconnected people are, and many young people find themselves shouting into the online void and accepting whatever answer comes back the loudest. It's easy to let ourselves be defined by others, without asking whether they know us or care about us at all. Teens and young adults, in particular, face many challenges that pierce the human heart, for example, how to navigate changing roles in the family, form new friendships, settle into a new living situation, or choose a vocation or a career. But few experiences are as profound—or as potentially confusing—as understanding our sexual identity and making sense of new and powerful desires for intimacy, connection, and love. Unfortunately, our secular culture does not offer much help: it tends to be *subjective* ("Truth is what I say it is"), *utilitarian* ("The best thing is the thing that gets me what I want"), and *hedonistic* ("The best thing is the thing that brings me the most pleasure"). If we ask the world, "What should I do with how I feel?" the answer comes back, "Do what you feel like, and what makes you feel good." We're no better off than before we asked the question!

And when what we're feeling is confusing already, a confused answer from the world doesn't help at all. Every young person feels sexual attractions—a desire to be intimate, physically and emotionally, with another person, to know and to belong to that person in a way that nobody else does. Sexual attractions are naturally oriented toward a person of the opposite sex, and they play a big part in making marriage and family possible and desirable. But some people, for various reasons, feel attractions for people of the same sex as themselves. This experience is difficult to understand and can leave them wondering what it means for their identity and for their future. Where can they turn to for answers when confused about their sexuality? The world seems to say that having sex is the most important experience people can have, that strong desires for connection are always sexual desires, that what they feel is always right, and that they always have to act on what they feel. Does an answer like this really help anybody?

Made for Love is an important answer to these questions about identity and sexuality. Like Saint Francis, Father Mike understands that the only real answer to the question "Who am I?" is to be found in the question "Who are you?"

I can only understand myself, that is, by understanding my relationships, especially my first and most important relationship, with my Creator. When I acknowledge God as Lord of my life, then I can call out to him: "O Lord, who are you?" His response is something I could never have expected: "I am your Father. I am your Savior. I am the source of your life. I am the destiny to which you are heading." When I know God's identity, I know my own more fully: "I am your beloved son. I belong to you. All that I have comes from you. All that I am is leading me to draw closer to you. I will listen to your Word and follow your plan for my life."

In his well-known conversational style, Father Mike writes about truths that everyone seemed to take for granted in the past, but that are downright revolutionary today:

- Your existence is a gift. It is good that you exist!
- Your body and soul are important.
- There's an objective truth behind everything, and you can understand it.
- Sex means something deeply important and has a specific purpose.
- Strong feelings don't always lead to good decisions.
- Friendship is real love and not a consolation prize.
- You can disagree with someone without hating the person.

Most of all, Father Mike knows what he's talking about, and he knows how you think. That knowledge, combined with his fatherly concern and compassion, means that *Made for Love* proclaims one message loud and clear: "You are who you are because God loves you!"

It's a privilege for me to work with men and women of many ages and backgrounds who are striving to understand their experience of same-sex attractions and respond as God invites them to do. More than ever, young people are facing the same challenge and striving to make the same response, and I am grateful that *Made for Love* is written with you in mind. As you come to understand God and his plan more deeply, I hope that you will also understand yourself and your desires better and live more fully as the person who God made you, in love, to be.

Father Philip G. Bochanski

Executive Director, Courage International

Introduction

"So...I'm gay."

The most important person in my life had called me the day before and told me that he wanted to drive up to Duluth, Minnesota, to talk. There we were, the next day, walking along the north shore of Lake Superior, and he was sharing one of the most personal details of his entire life with me.

What does a person say at a moment like that? What would you say or do if the person you loved most in the world bared his heart to you?

"Man...you know I love you." I hugged him, and he hugged me back. I was the third person he had ever told, and my very first instinct was to let him know that this new piece of information had changed nothing. We kept on walking, and he began to share his experience with me. He had always felt different. He had always had these stirrings, but he just did his best to ignore them or avoid thinking about them. But twenty-seven years is a long time to carry a secret that weighs so much, and he needed to let it out.

"Do you, um...do you have any questions?"

I thought it was really thoughtful of him to ask. I only had one question: "What are you going to do now?"

"What do you mean? I'm gay....I didn't choose to feel this way."

"I know. I know you didn't choose that...but what are you going to choose *now*?"

He wasn't sure, and I still don't know if he is sure, but this is "The Question" faced by every man or woman who experiences same-sex attractions.

I wrote this book for anyone who has been touched by the reality of same-sex attractions. If you have gone through life and have always felt different, if you are a parent of a child who has same-sex attractions, or if you love someone who experiences same-sex attractions, I wrote this book for you.

You do not have to be afraid of anything that you will find in this book, even if you have wrestled and struggled and fallen in the area of sexuality. The words of Jesus, spoken to a woman after she had been exposed for having fallen in the area of sexuality, are the underlying thread of this entire book. The scribes and Pharisees, wanting to entrap Jesus, asked if she should be stoned as commanded by the Law of Moses. Jesus replied, "Let him who is without sin among you be the first to throw a stone at her" (Jn 8:7). After the scribes and Pharisees had left, Jesus looked at the woman and said, "*Neither do I condemn you; go, and do not sin again*" (Jn 8:11; emphasis added). This encounter is great news for all of us. None of us is without sin, me definitely included. As John's Gospel says a few chapters earlier, "God sent the Son into the world, not to condemn the world, but that the world might be saved through him" (Jn 3:17). Jesus came not to condemn, but to save, to heal, to set right, to bring life. Even when he calls us to change, he does it so that we can be healed.

So you will find nothing in this book that is a personal condemnation. But that does not mean that this book will not be challenging. Following Christ is always challenging, but it is always possible and worth the effort. I have wrestled with the topic of same-sex attractions and the effects of this struggle on people close to me for over twenty-five years. I was very young when I realized that the experience of being attracted to the members of one's own sex would be a reality for many people I love. I was a committed Catholic Christian, and I knew that the Catholic Church had what some people would find to be challenging teachings in the area of sexuality. But I also knew that I might be called upon, one day, to offer a message of hope in the middle of what could seem to be a forest of *no's* and *don'ts*. From my personal experience, I knew that there would be a need for Catholics to understand where people who experience same-sex attractions were coming from. I knew that there would be guilt and shame and suspicion around the topic and that the Church would need many people to speak with a voice of compassion. And that is what I want this book to be.

This book is meant to explain *what* the Church teaches about same-sex attractions. It is also meant to explain *why* the Church teaches it. This book is for people who are affected by the experience of same-sex attractions. Above all, I want all those who read this book to know that same-sex attracted people do not have to make a "fool's choice"—a choice between two options, when *both* of them mean losing.

The fool's choice would be this: either you follow your heart, or you will be miserable. Either you indulge in what you desire, or you will be lonely. Either you accept and embrace everything that someone else chooses to do, or you hate and fear him. These are false options. Isn't there another way? Aren't there other choices? Isn't it possible to live out the teachings of Christianity and still be happy? Isn't it possible to love your neighbor and not agree with everything he chooses? I think there is a third choice. I think there is another way.

There Is a Third Way

Let's start at the beginning: *"It is good that you exist."* These need to be the first words that you hear. When God the Father sent Jesus to us, he was saying as loudly and clearly as he could to each one of us: It is good that you *are*. This world would be worse if you were not here.

I think of one of my best friends in college, Brian,[1] who was my little sister's Confirmation sponsor. Brian identifies as a gay man.[2] He is a nurse and has one of the most caring and compassionate hearts of anyone I have been privileged to know.

I think of a girl who sat across the center aisle of the church I attended while growing up. We rode the bus together all through elementary school. She identifies as a lesbian, and she advocates for those who have been made to feel out of place because of their sexual orientation.

---

[1] Names have been changed throughout this book to protect the privacy of those mentioned.

[2] Throughout this book, readers will encounter the terms "gay" and "lesbian." Catholics sometimes disagree about the appropriateness of these terms. Some object that the terms are widely used in a way that implies that a person is reducible to his sexual orientation or that this aspect of the person is the most significant one. Others object that the terms have connotations that fail to distinguish between mere same-sex attractions, on the one hand, and same-sex genital activity, on the other. Others insist that these terms ought to be used because many people choose to use them to describe themselves and that how people refer to themselves should be the determining factor in how other people speak of them. Here I use "gay" and "lesbian" when referring to how people describe themselves, without my use indicating endorsement or agreement with other people's intended use of the term. A number of people who identify as "gay" and "lesbian" have told me that their homosexual friends would take greater offense if I altogether refrained from these terms. On the other hand, some people will be offended or confused by their use, even in the limited form found herein.

I think of my former girlfriend, Melissa, who works with countless young men who have been cast out of their homes and now live on the streets, simply because they told their families that they were same-sex attracted.

I think of all of the young people I have worked with over the years. So many of them loved Jesus and loved the Church—but felt like they had no place in the Catholic Church because they identified as gay or lesbian.

I think of so many people who have reached out to me through the Internet, who are striving to live faithful, chaste lives but are afraid to reveal to their fellow Catholics that they are same-sex attracted.

I think of my best friend in the world, someone who calls himself a gay man, whom I have let drift away because I too often don't know what to say. My awkwardness is another indication that I sometimes see the "gay" and not the "man."

This is not to say that this is a book written out of guilt. It is written out of love. I do not want to reduce "love," as some Christians do, to mean: "I love you, so I need to tell you where you are wrong." I write this book because I know (I *know!*) that many people have experienced little love in the Catholic Church, especially when it comes to talking about same-sex attractions. People have often felt rejected, condemned, and unwanted.

In fact, it seems the more I talk with people, the clearer it becomes that many people in the Church could do a better job of communicating her teachings with love. I don't mean to say that the Church's teachings are not based in love. It is my strong conviction that all the directives Christ gives us lead to freedom and love. But there is a lot of confusion about what the Church teaches when it comes to sexuality in general and homosexuality in particular. Sometimes the love behind Church teaching is hard for people to see.

My goal is to provide some context to what the Church teaches regarding sexuality. But keep this in mind: This is the *beginning* of the discussion, not the end. I want to bring these issues up and do my best to explain the *what* and the *why* so that we all can have a starting point to begin speaking with each other. *With* each other, not *about* each other. There is a difference.

Too often, people like me in the Church will talk about *other people's* experiences with limited knowledge. I know *my* experience. And I know what people have shared with me. But I do not know *your* experience. And I realize that your experience might not be positive.

Still, in the course of this book, I don't always use examples from the lives of people who identify as gay or lesbian. The reason is because we all struggle with something. And we can approach the issues surrounding same-sex attractions in much the same way that we approach nearly all divisive issues. Focusing only on examples from people with same-sex attractions risks encouraging an "us versus them" outlook with some people. We can follow the path of dividing humanity into *us* and *them*. Or we can recognize that there is no *us* and *them*—there is only *us*. All of us are in the same situation.

To underscore the point, I want to say it again: It is good that you exist. You are one of "us."

A few people might find the very existence of this book offensive. I can understand that. I do not want to put into your hands just another "here is where you are wrong" kind of book. Consequently, I will do my best to be positive and affirmative. In fact, I want to affirm everything that I can affirm. Those who identify as gay have dignity. Those who experience same-sex attractions are worthwhile. Those who are grappling with their sexuality are part of the family, that is, part of the human family; and, if they are Christian, they are part of the family of God.

In short, if you are a same-sex attracted person, I want you to understand that when it comes to the Church, you belong here. There is more to say on how that should happen, but the affirmation that you should belong is something to be said before, during, and after everything else.

CHAPTER ONE

At the Beginning

A number of years ago, when I was a twenty-four-year-old seminarian in Saint Paul, Minnesota, I came home for a weekend break. As I dropped off my bag in my childhood bedroom, I noticed a picture book on my bed that I had never seen before. A couple of weeks before, my mom had gone to the funeral of a friend of hers, and, at the end of the service, someone got up and read from this children's book. The book was called *The Next Place*, and it was about life after death. My mom, knowing I would be presiding at a lot of funerals in the future, thought I might like a copy.

The book was pretty innocent and interesting. It had a number of harmless thoughts about what happens after a person dies. There were things that Catholics would agree with and embrace, such as the ideas that after death there would be a place of peace, that one would be reunited with loved ones, and that there would be no more suffering or sorrow—all nice things, of course.

But a couple of things gave me pause. The book stated, "My skin will not be dark or light. I won't be fat or tall. The body I once lived in won't be a part of me at all."[1] The author of the book went yet further and wrote this line as well: "I will

---

[1] Warren Hanson, *The Next Place* (Minneapolis, MN: Tristan, 1997).

not be a boy or a girl, a woman or man. I'll simply be just, simply, me."² Now, I understand that part of this is what death *is*—the separation of the soul from the body—but this author seemed to be taking his understanding of "the next place" to an entirely different level. While death is obviously marked by the separation of the soul from the body, the Judeo-Christian tradition has more to say about this. According to the Judeo-Christian view, human beings are a body-soul unity. In fact, the attempt to claim that the soul alone is the "true self" has been soundly condemned as heresy.

I walked down the stairs and into the kitchen, where my mom was reading a magazine. "Oh! Did you see that book I left on your bed?" she asked.

"I did."

"So, what did you think?"

"Ummm," I began, not knowing exactly how to express my disagreement but settling for the blunt truth. "It's heresy."

"What?" my mom exclaimed. "But I liked it!"

"Well, Mom, then I guess we have to agree that you're a heretic."

We had a laugh about that, but there was indeed a deeper problem with the book.

I completely understand the desire for the afterlife to be a place of bliss and peace, a place where we are free from the things that hold us back in this life, and a place where we are free of the things that we might not like about ourselves in this life (e.g., being tall or short, fat or thin, a boy or a girl). But the book gets one thing seriously wrong: our bodies are not "incidental" to who or what we are.

---

² Ibid.

In order to deal honestly about sexuality and the Catholic Church's teaching on how we can best live our lives as sexual beings, we need to start by answering a basic question: What is a human being?

Knowing *what* we are will go a long way toward revealing *who* we are and *how* we ought to live. If I don't know what a thing is, I will have a difficult time understanding it and a nearly impossible time knowing what is best for it.

Knowing what a human being is is the first step in knowing anything about ourselves. In the world of nutrition, when we understand the nature of man, we can understand best how to "fuel" ourselves. In the world of love, when we know what a human being is, we will know best how to love another.

Soul…and Body?

Most people have some sense that there is more to the human person than simply atoms and cells. Most of us have an intuition that there is more to the human mind than neurological pathways and chemical connections. We sense that these things are not *all* that a human person is. In Christian terminology, we also have *souls*. Now, just for a quick definition, the word "soul" in Latin is *anima*. The soul is what "animates" the body. It is not measurable, and it cannot be observed. But the *effects* of the soul are certainly observable. They are most strikingly visible in the difference between a living body and a dead body. If you have ever been in the presence of a person who has died, you know that there is something different, that something essential has been lost. Is it the mere fact that the heart is no longer beating or that the brain is no longer firing neurons? Possibly. But I think that there is something more. We recognize that the dead human body *seems* like an "empty shell." Without the soul, something is missing.

We say things such as, "That's not Dad," after seeing him at the funeral home. We can see that there has been a violation of the *integrity* of the person. I imagine that we would say a similar thing if we saw the ghost of a loved one; we would most likely say that we saw the "shadow" of the person—because a human being *is* a union of body and soul. Without the body, something is missing.

What Is Lazarus, Anyway?

If you are familiar with Scripture, I'm sure that you have heard the Parable of the Rich Man and Lazarus. With this parable, Jesus is teaching us how to treat others and how our actions in this life have an effect on our eternity:

> There was a rich man, who was clothed in purple and fine linen and who feasted sumptuously every day. And at his gate lay a poor man named Laz'arus, full of sores, who desired to be fed with what fell from the rich man's table; moreover the dogs came and licked his sores. The poor man died and was carried by the angels to Abraham's bosom. The rich man also died and was buried; and in Hades, being in torment, he lifted up his eyes, and saw Abraham far off and Laz'arus in his bosom. And he called out, "Father Abraham, have mercy upon me, and send Laz'arus to dip the end of his finger in water and cool my tongue; for I am in anguish in this flame." But Abraham said, "Son, remember that you in your lifetime received your good things, and Laz'arus in like manner evil things; but now he is comforted here, and you are in anguish. And besides all this, between us and you a great chasm has been fixed, in order that those who would pass from here to you may not be able, and none may cross from there to us." And he said, "Then I beg you, father, to send him to my father's house, for I have five brothers, so that he may warn them, lest they also come into this place of torment." But

Abraham said, "They have Moses and the prophets; let them hear them." And he said, "No, father Abraham; but if some one goes to them from the dead, they will repent." He said to him, "If they do not hear Moses and the prophets, neither will they be convinced if some one should rise from the dead." (Lk 16:19–31)

Now, as modern Westerners who have inherited the Christian view of things, we immediately know the point of this story. How *should* the rich man have treated Lazarus? He should have cared for him, right? He should have done what many followers of Jesus have done throughout history. He should *not* merely have stepped over Lazarus, but he should have acted on behalf of this suffering man, and done his best to help Lazarus live. But how might someone with a different worldview look at Lazarus?

Different Worldviews Are Actually, Well, Different

Let's briefly consider three different ways of looking at the world and at the human person. Not all religions teach the same thing, and not all people believe the same thing about what a human being is. How would a Hindu look at Lazarus? How about a Buddhist? How would an atheist look at Lazarus? What do these three different worldviews believe about *what* Lazarus is? I want to look at these beliefs and see how they hold up under scrutiny.

The Hindu View of a Human Person

Let's imagine that a wealthy Hindu living in Bombay were to approach Lazarus. This poor man is lying in the gutter covered with sores. He has no family or job; he is one of "the untouchables." Therefore, being a Hindu, what *ought* the rich man do when he sees Lazarus?

Surprisingly (to us), he should do exactly what the man in the parable did! He *ought* to avoid contact with the poor man. He ought not to touch him. This is where the traditional name *untouchables* comes from. What might explain this kind of behavior? It has to do with the Hindu understanding of human nature. How we view the nature of the human person will determine how we treat the human person.

From a Hindu point of view, Lazarus is a soul trapped in a body. Lazarus is not his body, and the body is not Lazarus. Lazarus is merely his soul. His fate is to live out his *karma* in this body until the body dies and his soul is reincarnated (i.e., gets a new body, and not necessarily a human one) repeatedly until he attains oneness with the Atman.

Once I was speaking with a young Hindu man, and he affirmed this idea. He gave me the following example: Imagine you are taking a road trip from New York to California, but your car breaks down in Iowa. You don't abandon your trip. Instead, you simply acquire a new car and keep going. Even if your car kept breaking down and you had to get several new cars, the "real you" would continue traveling. But (and this is key) you are not the car; the car is merely the shell that helps you get where you are going.

So for Hindus, people are souls trapped in bodies; their bodies are not an essential part of who they are.

The Buddhist View of a Human Person

Gautama Buddha was raised Hindu, and it seems that he had become disillusioned with the notion of having an untouchable class. This moved him to do something to understand the sources of suffering in the world.

According to Gautama Buddha, in order to eliminate suffering, it is necessary to discover the origins of suffering and to then pull it out from the roots. Buddha saw that suffering comes from unfulfilled desire. We all know how this works; we want something, but we can't have it. I want sleep, but I have to stay up and study. I want food, but I have to wait until dinner. I desire to be in close relationship with someone, but I am alone. These different experiences of human suffering can all be traced back to unfulfilled desire.

Further, desire itself has a source. Buddha asked, "*Who is doing the desiring?*" The answer is, "The self." The person. The "I." If the individual is the source of desire, and desire is the source of suffering, then the individual is the source of suffering. In order to eliminate suffering, one had to eliminate unfulfilled desire. But, so it is thought, to eliminate unfulfilled desire, one needed to eliminate the source of desire: the self.

This current of thought gave rise to the Buddhist notion that the self is an illusion, not a real thing. This view extended to the belief that the entire material world is merely an illusion. While not every Buddhist tradition teaches this radical perspective of "material reality as unreal," it is the one originally taught by Gautama.

So while a Hindu would say that Lazarus is a soul trapped in a body, a Buddhist would say that Lazarus is neither a soul nor body; his individuality is ultimately an illusion. If you have ever seen the movie *The Matrix*, you are familiar with the idea that what we think of as the real world and even what constitutes ourselves is an illusion. In that movie, human beings' consciousness is linked to a computer program created by some kind of artificial intelligence. They perceive themselves as bodies, walking around in a real world, but they are actually living in pods. Virtually all of what they perceive as reality is simply a fabrication. Yet if they are willing to take the "blue pill," they can be set free; they can leave the world of illusions and achieve "Enlightenment."

In that kind of world, "waking" the un-Enlightened would be a gesture of compassion. In fact, it would be the greatest act of compassion one could do for another. The rich man, if he was Enlightened, would best help Lazarus by helping him realize that he doesn't exist in the sense that he thinks he does and that all the world is merely an illusion.

We saw how for a Hindu, Lazarus was a soul without a body. For a Buddhist, Lazarus is neither a soul nor a body.

The Atheist View of a Human Person

Finally, how would an atheist see Lazarus?

As you know, an atheist is someone who believes that there is no God. Atheists usually hold that all that exists is some version of "matter." In other words, most honest atheists are strict materialists. According to this view of things, there is no spirit or soul; there is only the material world. Therefore, an atheist would say that Lazarus is a body without a soul. Lazarus is simply a certain collection of protons, neutrons, and electrons, and nothing more.

Atheism is both the most problematic and the simplest worldview. It is the most problematic for at least two reasons. First, if there is no God, then it is difficult to see how there can be any "oughts."

Consider it this way: If there is no God who created all that is, and yet the universe exists, then it exists for no reason or purpose, since reason and purpose are qualities that attach only to a conscious mind. The universe is therefore ultimately an accident. All of existence is random. A universe without a Creator is necessarily a universe without meaning. In a universe with no meaning, there cannot be a right and wrong, only preferences and utility. That means that there is no good or evil, but merely what I like and will, and what works.

If an atheist reached out and helped Lazarus, it would only be because either he happened to feel like it at the moment, or because he found it useful to him according to some scheme or other. There might be some actions that are more or less useful than others in an atheist view, but there could be no obligation to help, or not help, anyone. If an atheist preferred a notion like the common good over self-preservation, that person might choose to help Lazarus because it would be useful to advance that particular preference.

Secondly, if there is nothing more to Lazarus than there is to any other carbon-based life form, then treatment could take any variety of methods. If Lazarus was nothing more than his body, then we could treat him with the same kind of compassion with which we treat other kinds of animals. If your dog suffered to the same degree as Lazarus did, how would you care for him? Out of love for your dog, you might very well put him to sleep. You would gently and compassionately euthanize your dog as a kindness. If Lazarus is not substantially different from your dog, then this would be a reasonable option for how to care for a human being, an option that many in our society are beginning to choose.

Now I'm not suggesting that all atheists are immoral people who care about nothing except their own preference and convenience. Obviously, there are very kind and generous atheists. There are even times when atheists may seem to show more kindness and love than Christians. What I do want to suggest is that this kindness or generosity on the part of an atheist doesn't follow from the atheist worldview. Atheists who live according to moral standards do so despite their atheistic philosophy, not because of it.

So here are three distinct worldviews: the Hindu sees the human person as a soul trapped in a body; the Buddhist sees the human person as neither a body nor a soul; and the atheist views the human person as a body without a soul. Depending on the view one takes, there will be different and important consequences concerning how people are treated in the real world.

So, what is a human being? Are we just bodies? Are we just souls? Or are we just nothing?

The Christian View of a Human Person

There is yet another view, the Christian one. And it is this: You and everyone you have ever met are created in the image and likeness of God. Every human being has a unique and rational soul that animates his human body. In the Christian view, humans are both bodies *and* souls.

Some Christians mistakenly believe they are destined to be angels. This is the idea found in the classic Christmas movie *It's a Wonderful Life*. While that is a sweet idea, human beings don't become angels when they die. We know this for a number of reasons.

Angels are spiritual beings; they don't have bodies. Human beings differ from them in a very important way: human beings do have bodies. Christians believe that each of us is a unity of body and soul. As I noted earlier, a human body without a soul is a corpse, and a human soul without a body is a ghost. When we die we will remain human. This means that, ultimately, we will have both a body and a soul in the resurrection of the dead.

What does that tell us? For one thing, it tells us that Christians believe that the body is good! In fact, the body is at the heart of the Christian faith. God chose to save the world by means of a human nature, including a human body. "The Church calls 'Incarnation' the fact that the Son of God assumed a human nature in order to accomplish our salvation in it" (*Catechism of the Catholic Church*, no. 461). The root of the word "incarnation" comes from the Latin word *caro*, which means "flesh." Therefore, incarnation essentially means "en-*flesh-ment*." The Son of God took on a human nature, which includes a human body, and through his life, suffering, death, and Resurrection in that body, he saved the world.

Because of this, Christians believe that the body is good! One of the early Christian writers, a man named Tertullian, went so far as to write, "The flesh is the hinge of salvation"![3] This is a big deal!

There have been times when Christians were accused of believing that the body was a "necessary evil." But that has never been the teaching of the Catholic Church. The truth is that the body is at the heart of Catholic life and worship. Catholics believe that the Eucharist is truly the Body, Blood, Soul, and Divinity of Jesus—and that the Eucharist is among the greatest gifts we have received from God. Even more, Catholics are not merely called to think about the Eucharist or spiritually to receive the Body of Christ without bodily action; Jesus tells us to "eat" and "drink" (Jn 6:53).

There's more! Christianity makes the claim that your body is an essential part of who you are. Because human beings are a unity of body and soul, and because the body is good, this means that at the end of the ages when the final story is told, those who attain the fullness of life in Heaven will receive

---

[3] Tertullian, *De Resurrectione Carnis (On the Resurrection of the Body)*, 8, 2 (*PL* 2, 852).

their bodies in perfect form. If you're a man, like Jesus you'll be a man forever. If you're a woman, like Mary you'll be a woman forever. What difference does that make? It makes a huge difference! If you are your body and your soul, then what you do with your body matters. This is just common sense. If you rejoice with your body, then it is *you* rejoicing. If you suffer with your body, then it is *you* suffering. If you sin with your body, then it is *you* sinning. This is what Pope Saint John Paul II meant when he said, "The body, and it alone, is capable of making visible the invisible... the spiritual and the divine."[4] The only way you and I have ever known anything or anyone has been through the body! Understanding the importance of our bodies for who we are makes a difference for how we are able to proceed from here on out.

If your body is not an essential part of who you are, then you can use it however you want, like a tool. But if your body is a vital aspect of who you are, then what you do with your body *matters*.

---

[4] John Paul II, *Man and Woman He Created Them: A Theology of the Body* (Boston: Pauline, 2006), 76.

CHAPTER TWO

What-It-Is-Ness

How do we understand the world around us?

This question is connected to a concept we call *nature*. Philosophically speaking, the nature of a thing is what could be called its *what-it-is-ness*. (Philosophers sometimes use the fancy word "quiddity.") Knowing the what-it-is-ness of something is not just for philosophers; it is for everyone. If we are going to treat or use a thing well, we need to know what it is—we need to know its nature.

Remember the last time someone asked you to define something, something that stumped you. Maybe you used a term or referred to something, and someone asked, "What is that?" You *knew* what it was, but you couldn't come up with a definition that would adequately describe the thing. For example, if someone were to ask you, "What is time?" you could say *something* about time, but you might find it hard to offer an actual definition of time. It's kind of like what Supreme Court Justice Stewart said about obscenity: "I shall not today attempt further to define [it] ... and perhaps I could never succeed in intelligibly doing so. But I know it when I see it."[1]

---

[1] Jacobellis v. Ohio, 11 S. Ct. (1964), http://caselaw.findlaw.com/us-supreme-court/378/184.html.

While that might be a clever answer—and even an honest answer—it isn't a helpful answer. What is helpful is to know what a thing *is*. This isn't always clear and straightforward, but it's very important because if we can't state what a thing *is*, then there is no way to know how to treat it.

We can begin to perceive the nature of a thing by discerning its purpose, or *end*. In other words, we can understand the what-it-is-ness of a thing by discovering the what-it-is-*for*-ness.

What-It-Is-For-Ness

Consider this simple example: a chair. What is the end of a chair? The what-it-is-for-ness is to sit on. A chair is that specific kind of a thing that is created to sit on, and this is the case for all chairs. There are many different kinds of chairs, made from any number of different materials and using any number of different styles and shapes and colors. There are folding chairs, recliner chairs, pub-style chairs, desk chairs, barber chairs, and so forth. But while there are many different *kinds* of chairs, they all share the same nature of *chair-ness* because they all share the same end: they are for sitting on.

The same thing could be said about any number of things. Think of a table. What is the nature of a table? Well, what is the what-it-is-for-ness of a table? The end or purpose of a table is that people might set things on it. Despite the variations of materials and styles, sizes, and shapes, all tables share in one nature: *table-ness*.

Now, knowing the intrinsic end of a chair or table, I can use them according to their what-it-is-for-ness. (I sit on a chair and set things on a table.) But have you ever sat on a table? I'm sure you have. Have you ever placed something on a chair? Of course, we do that kind of thing all the time. So what we have is a potential mini-conflict. We can know the end or purpose for which a thing was made, but yet we might use it for an end or purpose of our own. Does this cause any real conflict? Sometimes not or not much. For example, if you sit on a table, you're acting a bit at odds with the purpose of a table—which isn't to sit on but to set things on. Sometimes a somewhat different use of a thing isn't radically at odds with its what-it-is-for-ness.

Is It All Good?

Let's keep going. What is the nature of an ax? The end, or what-it-is-for-ness, of the ax is "to chop." Someone could use the ax to chop wood, or to kill an innocent person. Would it violate the nature of the ax if it was used to kill someone who was innocent? No. The person would not be violating the what-it-is-for-ness of the ax, but he would still be doing something evil.

On one hand, we can use a thing for its proper end (e.g., placing glasses, plates, and silverware on a table), and we can use it for a different end (e.g., sitting on a table), in both cases preserving the thing's nature, even if one use is better suited than another to it. On the other hand, we can use a thing in accord with its nature but for an evil purpose (e.g., killing someone with an ax).

But are there times when people could use a thing for their own purposes in such a way that violates the nature of that thing? Of course there are.

If we were to use a table as a ramp for my car so we could get underneath and change the oil, would we violate the nature of the table? I think so, and relatively quickly. If we used a chair as a stand for splitting wood, would we violate the nature of the chair? Of course. If we used an ax to drive in railroad spikes, would we violate its nature? Yes, and, as a result, the integrity of the ax would disintegrate.

It is possible to use a thing in such a way that violates the very nature of that thing. When we do this, there are always negative consequences. We can't dodge those consequences forever. We may ignore them for a time or try to lessen their effects. But that is only temporary.

All of this is to say that everything has an *end*. There is a purpose to creation.

It's Only Human Nature

When it comes to being human, there is such a thing as human nature. While human beings often look different from each other in many ways, we share in the same nature—*human nature*. While one could use that term to refer to "how" human beings experience this life, in a deeper sense it means that there is an *end* to every human being. There is a purpose to every human life. There is a *what-it-is-for-ness*.

Christ teaches that there is a destiny for which you have been created. There is a purpose and a reason that you are alive. Christians believe that our end, our purpose, and our goal is to be an image of God to this world, and to live forever with God in Heaven. We are intended to know, love, and serve God in this world in such a way as to live with him forever in the next.[2] The body-soul unity that we discussed earlier is also part of our human nature. Therefore, what we do with our bodies makes a difference. Our actions have consequences. Some are obvious, while others are subtle. Here's a quick little example: Say that you head to the break room every workday about 10:15 A.M. Your office break

---

[2] *Baltimore Catechism No. 1*, answer to question no. 6, "Why did God make you?"

room is awesome; it's always stocked with doughnuts. So you start eating a doughnut every day. Soon, this physical action will manifest itself in a physical way. Not only will there be consequences *to your body*, but there will also be hidden consequences—something will happen in your mind as well. You will find yourself "needing" the doughnut. Not that your body actually needs the nourishment that the doughnut provides (you can try convincing yourself that!), but your mind will think you do. Something inside you will have changed. Your mind will have changed. Your habits will have changed. Our physical actions can have nonphysical consequences. If our bodies are an essential part of who we are, then what we do with our bodies matters.

While we are made for a purpose, we can choose to live "on purpose" or "off purpose." If we live in accordance with our human nature, our lives have integrity, and things tend to go well. If we live in violation of our nature, we tend to become disintegrated, and we fail to live fully.

So, let's get down to it. Sex. This is a very important and, ultimately, *human* action.

Birds Do It . . .

Some may argue that all animals engage in sexual reproduction, and, therefore, nothing is specifically "human" about the sexual act. But human beings are not mere "animals"; we are "persons." We have been given rational minds that seek out what is true; and we have rational wills that look out for what is good. This means that human actions differ from other animal actions. We are what are called moral agents. This means that we can choose to do the right thing, or we can choose to do the wrong thing. Animals cannot choose to do right or wrong—at least not in the full sense of choosing right or wrong. We accept this as common sense; there has never been a criminal trial for a monkey.

A recent article in *Time* magazine stated, "Infanticide is disturbingly common in nature."[3] I find this *statement* disturbing. How could an animal action be described as "disturbing"? Animals are not moral agents. They cannot discern right from wrong in the same way that human beings do. Animals may be capable of acts that we *anthropomorphize* or talk about as if they had been done by a human being. We might call such acts "disturbing" or "heroic," while recognizing the difference between how animals are spoken of as acting in this way and how human beings do. For example, a dog can rescue its owner, but the act is not "heroic"; it is merely instinctual. Of course, I'm glad dogs can rescue people, but I don't expect an animal to act morally in the same way that I expect another human person to act morally. Similarly, if an animal does something to harm people, we don't attribute moral blame to the animal, as we often do to human beings.

When it comes to sex, many people will argue that, if some kind of sexual behavior occurs among animals, it must be "natural" for humans too. This assertion fails for the same reason. Animals and humans share many similar characteristics, but we differ in one essential way: we are moral agents and they are not. Animals do not dwell in the world of right or wrong; we do. The fact that certain sexual patterns are found in animal behavior—whether they may seem attractive to us like having multiple partners, or repulsive to us like coercive sex—is no more a justification

---

[3] Jeffrey Kluger, "Scientists Rush to Understand the Murderous Mamas of the Monkey World," *Time*, June 15, 2011.

for human sexual behavior than infanticide among animals is a pointer to how we should treat our young.

The Nature of the Sexual Act

So how should we understand the human sexual act? What does human nature have to say about the matter?

If aliens were sent to Earth to study human sexual behavior, they would quickly recognize that the human action of the sexual embrace is an expression of something important about human nature. Regardless of the many ways various people might use it for their own purposes, sex has an intrinsic meaning and a very clear what-it-is-for-ness linked to human what-it-is-for-ness.

Objectively speaking, the sexual act is oriented toward two *ends*: the complementary union of the couple (also called the "unitive end") and procreation.

Studies have shown that an emotional and chemical bond is formed during the sexual embrace. While there is an abundance of anecdotal evidence to support this, there is also medical evidence. For example, when a couple enters into the sexual embrace, a chemical compound called oxytocin is released into the bloodstream. The release of *this* chemical at *this* moment is not incidental; it is oriented toward bonding the couple. For men, oxytocin is released at climax, which, even physiologically, links the procreative and unitive ends of the sexual act. Oxytocin is also the same chemical that is released when a woman breastfeeds her child; it is oriented toward bonding the mother and child.

In addition to whatever emotional and chemical bonds that sexual acts tend to form, there is also a moral bond we should keep in mind. In sexual relations, as we said earlier, a person "gives himself" to another, who in turn "receives him." And the other "gives herself" to him, who in turn "receives her." They "gift" themselves one to another, mutually "giving" and "receiving" one another through this deeply personal action of uniting their bodies through their sexual organs. The two "become one flesh" as the Bible says, forming a complementary unity, one that is by its nature oriented to bringing new human beings into existence. Indeed, in this sense, it a mutual union in which the couple holds nothing back in their sexual act from each other.

Which brings us to the other "end" of sex, which is perhaps even more obvious. The sexual act is the particular human act oriented toward the procreation of children. We moderns, it is true, have been largely successful at separating the sexual act from the conception of children. But the biological fact remains that the act of sexual intercourse between a man and a woman is the only act that naturally results in the creation of new human life.

The Intention of an Action

When we talk about the "what-it-is-for-ness" of some ability we have as human beings—such as our sexual organs to form a complementary union open to new life and to procreate, or the power of eyes to see or the ears to hear—we distinguish between the inherent or "built-in" purpose or good to be achieved by the activity of our bodily organs and their ability or power, on the one hand, and whatever particular purpose we may have in mind, on the other. Since our natural abilities are things God gave us in order to fulfill ourselves as persons, we should respect those abilities and not use them in harmful ways. This is where a link between our "what-it-is-for-ness" and what we intend or seek to do, comes in. If we intend to use an ability in a way that harms us (even if we don't think it will), then there is a disconnect between that ability's "what-it-is-for-ness" and our intention or purpose. That makes our purpose contrary to God's purpose in giving us this ability in the first place.

What if a person intentionally ate food for pleasure, but then, in order to prevent nourishment, chose to make himself vomit? Pleasure, which often accompanies the proper exercise of our abilities, including the ability to eat, shouldn't be sought in a way that disrespects or opposes the reason we have our natural abilities. Many of us know someone for whom eating is a very serious issue. For many different reasons, a number of people struggle with this problem to the point where after eating, they must purge themselves. And they do this because they believe that they will be happier for it. If you know and love a person who experiences this, you wouldn't tell him, "I understand that this is your battle, so I will not try to help you heal." Would you be content if he only violated the nature of eating "on occasion"? Not at all. This isn't just because there is some kind of rule that states, "We ought not violate the nature of eating." There is a reason that goes much deeper.

We perceive that working against the natural purpose of eating negatively affects the *person*. Since the body is an essential part of the person, what someone does with the body matters. And working against something as simple and basic as eating can have real effects on a person; if we violate the integrity of the act of eating, we can inflict damage on the person.

Let's Talk About Sex (Again)

Sex, too, is a human act with an objective natural purpose. Knowing that there are two *ends* of the sexual embrace—unity and procreation—could a couple come together with only one of these *ends* in mind? Sure they could. You can imagine a husband and wife entering into the sexual embrace for the *purpose* of intimacy, for the *purpose* of unity. They don't have to also have the intention or *purpose* of conceiving a child. Likewise, I know many couples who have struggled with infertility. For them, after visits with doctors and other health care professionals, they might have an increased awareness of when the woman is most likely to be able to conceive. In those cases, it is imaginable that the couple might enter into the sexual embrace with the *purpose* of procreation. They might not be intending intimacy at that particular moment, and they could do this without violating the integrity of the sexual act.

But what if they intentionally worked against one of the *ends* of the sexual act? Is it possible for the couple to violate the integrity of the sexual act by preventing either *end*?

Absolutely it is.

If a person intentionally worked against the *unitive end* of the sexual embrace, what do we call that? Sometimes, in extreme cases, it's called sexual assault or rape, but most of the time it's the selfish using of another person.

If a person intentionally worked against the *procreative end* of the sexual embrace, what do we call that? We call it contraception: entering into a sexual act with the intention of preventing procreation. In other words, contraception violates the inherent nature of the sexual act.

And there are consequences to the *person*.

Are You Serious?

When speaking to college students on this idea, some of them will eventually get to the point where they will blurt out, "I don't understand why you are making such a big deal about sex. It isn't anything special; it's just something nice to do."

If that is true, then the executive producer Dick Wolf is terribly mistaken, as are millions of TV viewers. Dick Wolf produces one of the most-watched television crime dramas ever: *Law & Order*. While there are a number of spin-offs from the original *Law & Order*, one of the most successful is *Law & Order: SVU*. The "SVU" stands for "Special Victims Unit." As the narrator states in the voice-over at the beginning of each episode:

> In the criminal justice system, sexually based offenses are considered especially heinous. In New York City, the dedicated detectives who investigate these vicious felonies are members of an elite squad known as the Special Victims Unit. These are their stories.

In this introduction, it appears that sex is a big deal and special. Why else would sexually based offenses be considered "especially heinous"? It is because the sexual act is something that intimately concerns the *person*. This is why rape is a more severe crime than mugging. We know that sexual crimes are inherently more damaging than other crimes such as theft. It's so obvious that it would be willful ignorance to deny the drastic distinction between the two. So why would we pretend that sex doesn't deeply affect a person? One possible reason is that some people may attempt to downplay the significance of sex so that they can do what they want.

If we tell ourselves that sex is "no big deal," or that it "doesn't mean anything," then we give ourselves permission to do whatever we want when it comes to sex. At the end of the day, however, if the nature of the sexual act is violated, we end up harming ourselves and others. We can't avoid the consequences of undermining the natural purpose of sex by simply believing there's nothing special about it; there exists an objective nature to sex that cannot be molded to our own subjective outlooks.

Fractured Sex, Fractured People, Fractured Relationships

So here's the principle: because the sexual act is rooted in our human nature and has a purpose related to that nature, if we act in such a way as to violate that nature, we do damage to ourselves and others. We tend to disintegrate.

And our culture has witnessed this disintegration. In the years since artificial contraception became readily available, many couples have intentionally removed the procreative aspect of the sexual embrace. At the same time, there has been a steep escalation in the divorce rate, sexual abuse, pornography, abortion, and homosexual behavior, as well as an increase in the abandonment of children.

In her book *Adam and Eve after the Pill: Paradoxes of the Sexual Revolution*, noted author and researcher Mary Eberstadt points to the overwhelming statistical evidence that shows the correlation between artificial contraception and these societal problems. For example, she notes how Nobel Prize–winner George Akerlof demonstrated, "using the language of modern economics, why the sexual revolution . . . had led to an increase in both illegitimacy and abortion."[4] In an article for *First Things* magazine, Eberstadt further describes how Akerlof connects these changes with the "rise in poverty and social pathology."[5]

---

[4]　Mary Eberstadt, *Adam and Eve after the Pill: Paradoxes of the Sexual Revolution* (San Francisco: Ignatius Press, 2012), 137–38. Eberstadt was referring to George A. Akerlof, Janet L. Yellen, and Michael L. Katz, "An Analysis of Out-of-Wedlock Childbearing in the United States," *Quarterly Journal of Economics* 111, no. 2 (1996): 277–317.

[5]　Mary Eberstadt, "The Vindication of *Humanae Vitae*," *First Things*, August 2008, https://www.firstthings.com/article/2008/08/002-the-vindication-of-ihu-manae-vitaei.

All of Us

These issues affect all of us, not just married people, not just divorced people, not just single people—and not just people who experience same-sex attractions.

Even though we are all tempted at various times, we are made for truth and love. One of the reasons we don't love well is that we don't have a good idea of what love really is.

CHAPTER THREE

Search Your Feelings....
You Know It to Be True

In 2005, sociologist Christian Smith conducted a nationwide survey on the spiritual lives of American adolescents. The results of that survey revealed a great deal about what American teens *really* believe when it comes to their faith. Smith's survey involved young people from a variety of faith backgrounds, including self-professed atheists. When he asked young people about the kind of God that they believed in, he was shocked by their responses.

First, regardless of their faith background, most teens professed some kind of faith in the same kind of "god." Second, this god was one that virtually none of the established, creedal religions professed to exist.[1]

---

[1] Christian Smith, *Soul Searching: The Religious and Spiritual Lives of American Teenagers* (Oxford: Oxford University Press, 2005). Smith called the emerging belief system held by American adolescents "MTD": Moralistic, Therapeutic Deism. He described MTD in brief as asserting these five beliefs: "1. A god exists who created and ordered the world and watches over human life on earth; 2. God wants people to be good, nice, and fair to each other, as taught in the Bible and by most world religions; 3. The central goal of life is to be happy and to feel good about oneself; 4. God does not need to be particularly involved in one's life except when He is needed to resolve a problem; 5. Good people go to heaven when they die."

In 2011, Christian Smith published his findings about the moral lives of American young adults. He was interested in discovering how these young adults made moral decisions. How did they resolve conflict? To what degree did their beliefs guide their actions and choices?

What he found was remarkable. Most of these young adults had virtually no sense of how to make moral decisions. In fact, Smith concluded that the majority of American young adults have neither the *ability* nor the *categories* to make moral decisions.

I know this sounds shocking (because it is!). In his research, most of the young adults didn't even consider themselves to be "moral actors." Smith reports, "Two-thirds of the emerging adults we interviewed (about 66 percent) proved simply unable to engage our questions about moral dilemmas in their lives."[2]

Without any clear "moral sense," they did not view themselves as having ever made a moral decision. Their answers included such things as, "I don't really know, 'cause I've never had to make a decision about what's right and what's wrong," and, "Nothing really is coming to mind. I haven't had too many really huge moral dilemmas that I've had to navigate through in my lifetime, I don't think. Nothing is coming to mind right now."[3]

Further, when asked how they might resolve a moral conflict, many of those asked didn't have any standard by which they could make consistent or wise choices. "I don't know. . . . It's just a feeling, I guess." *Feelings* tended to be one of the consistent criteria for making decisions. But ten seconds

---

[2] Christian Smith, *Lost in Transition: The Dark Side of Emerging Adulthood* (Oxford: Oxford University Press, 2011), 59.

[3] Ibid., 55.

of reflection on this should reveal how inconsistent and fickle feelings are; much more is needed than "how does this make me feel?" Without an objective standard, not only is there no way to assess the rightness or wrongness of a decision, but there is also no way to grow in wisdom. A person who uses only feelings as the basis for decision-making remains a slave to preference or mood.

It should be easy to see why Smith concluded that many people do not have the ability to make a moral decision. Ability demands *awareness* of when one is faced with a moral decision. It further demands a process that goes beyond "feeling." Without any kind of objective standard, an individual can only base decisions on subjective desires or anticipated outcomes. Without any clear reference point for what is right or wrong, morality boils down to either utility or preference.

As I pointed out in chapter two, a world without God is a world without purpose. Without a designer, there is no inherent design. Without an intentional beginning, there is no intentional *end*. Without God, there is no wrong or right. Instead, decisions are based on criteria such as obtaining our own goals or personal preferences. Many people claim to subscribe to this idea, but few are willing to follow the idea to its logical conclusion. If people did so, they would quickly realize that what they believe can't be reconciled with their experience of reality.

Years ago, I read about a man who had taken his teenage children and their friends to the movie *Schindler's List*. If you are unfamiliar with the film, it is a powerful and heart-wrenching depiction of the treatment that Jews and others experienced in Nazi concentration camps. The protagonist, Oskar Schindler, was a nominal Catholic man who filled the Nazis' need for munitions with his factories, causing him to become wealthy and successful. In the course of the story, he has a change of heart and can no longer ignore the persecution of those in the concentration camps. This change of heart leads him to save the lives of hundreds of Jews.

After the man and the teens saw the movie, they went out for pizza. The man was interested in finding out what they thought about the movie, so he began gently probing them with questions about it.

"What did you think about what Schindler did? What might it have been like to be one of those parents in the concentration camp? What do you think you would have done if you were in Oskar Schindler's position? What was the most powerful scene in the movie for you?"

After the teens shared their thoughts and feelings on the questions above, the man asked, "Was what the Nazis did to those people in the concentration camps *wrong*?" Almost immediately, and unanimously, all of the teens agreed that it was wrong.

Next, he asked them, "*Why* was it wrong?" This question left them all speechless; they didn't know how to answer it. Despite the fact that the teenagers didn't immediately know how to answer the question, the man didn't give up pressing them for an answer. Eventually, one of the teens responded, "I don't know. . . . It just made me *feel* bad."

The Barna Group conducted a 2002 study that revealed a staggering statistic: 94 percent of young Americans claimed to reject the idea of absolute right and wrong.[4] This means that the vast majority of young Americans are

---

[4] "Americans Are Most Likely to Base Truth on Feelings," Barna Research Group, February 12, 2002, www.barna.com/research/americans-are-most-likely-to-base-truth-on-feelings/.

unwilling to say simply that there are some actions that are always and everywhere wrong. Whether that is true in practice is doubtful, but it tells us something about the moral atmosphere that surrounds us. The overwhelming majority opinion concerning morality seems to be that it's relative.

The conclusion of this line of reasoning is somewhat obvious: If there is no such thing as absolute truth or an objective right and wrong, then the only reason a thing is wrong is that it makes me feel bad. Conversely, if a thing seems to make me feel good, then it must be "good," right?

Now I acknowledge that people may not really think this way in all aspects of life. They admit that in certain areas some things are always wrong, even if they tend to talk as if "everything is relative." Most people would acknowledge such things as racism and rape are always wrong. They would probably also acknowledge that someone should follow a certain judgment of conscience. That is, if someone really thinks something is wrong, that person shouldn't do it. Yet when it comes to sexuality, many people adopt a relativistic stance. We might ask whether this is because to admit that when it comes to sex, there are some definite and final "rights" and "wrongs" that tend to interfere with what people want to do. And sex is such a deep part of most of us that many people insist on doing what they want to do in this area, even if on a certain level they know or suspect that what they want to do may be wrong. Adopting an attitude of "everything is relative" when sex is involved seems to make things easier— at least if we don't think too much about it.

Have We Forgotten How to Argue?

You can see how it is difficult to have a rational conversation about morality in this kind of culture. If there are objective standards for right and wrong, then it is possible to have a real debate about morality. People can argue passionately *and* rationally about right and wrong, and make progress. But if I am the source of right and wrong, another person cannot argue against my ideas without attacking me because I am the source of my truth. Therefore, to critique my opinion and say that it is wrong is to attack me and say that there is something wrong with me.

I have found this to be the case when I discuss issues with high school and college students. People don't like to be challenged, or corrected, or told that they are wrong. But when we slip into thinking of ourselves as the source of truth, to be told that we are wrong is not merely to be told that we hold a wrong viewpoint; it is to be told that we are wrong in a much deeper sense.

When reality is considered something outside, or *independent*, of oneself, one can debate the nature of reality with another person. When truth is understood as something discovered and not as something "invented," then two or more people can talk about it, argue about it, and even change their minds about it. But in an age where truth is often reduced to subjective truth, I can only share *my* subjective opinion and listen to *your* subjective opinion. This is the current breakdown of the moral argument and moral reasoning.

"Don't Judge Me"

I hear this statement all the time. And I understand it; no one likes to be judged. Isn't it interesting, though, how we live in a culture in which so many things are permissible or excusable, and yet everyone is terrified of being judged. Why is that?

One fall day, a couple of years ago, I was talking with one of my brother's colleagues, an intelligent and no-nonsense military officer. We were speaking about getting older and how the culture around us seemed to be changing so quickly. He and I are roughly the same age, and the differences we saw between the world we were raised in and the world today were similar. At a certain point in our conversation, the officer said, "Oh, well. My dad said the same things about the world changing, too. Maybe because people are living longer now they're able to notice more significant changes than earlier generations."

I considered this idea for a moment. Could that be it? Has it *always* been the case that older people *always* look at the younger generation and lament such significant changes? I don't think so.

While leaving room for a generous amount of self-deception—we often are good at "self-editing" our memories of what our youth was really like—I think that the last few generations have seen (not merely perceived) more actual change than previous generations. Some historians of culture have suggested that there have been three main epochs in human cultural history: premodern (prehistory to the 1500s), modern (1500s–1960), and postmodern (1960–present). While this is not the only possible way to divide history, it will be useful for our purposes in trying to shed light on some of the "macro" developments that have occurred. In particular, these eras are distinguished by the way people of their times perceived the source of truth.

Living in the premodern world largely involved accepting reality as one found it. Philosophy and religion were rooted in the human attempt to make sense of and understand the nature of the universe. The chief task was to "discover" the meaning of existence. In the premodern era, truth was understood to inhere in God and in created reality, and therefore truth was considered objective.

The modern world was marked with the introduction of a new kind of science and technology. Man began to wonder if certain elements of the natural world were not merely discoverable but also controllable. Having gained increasing control over material reality, people wondered whether all aspects of reality had some potential to be manipulated.

René Descartes, the father of modern philosophy, turned centuries of philosophical reasoning on its head when he began to challenge the a priori assumptions of the medieval world. He began his paradigm-shifting work, *Discourse on Method*, with the determination to doubt all that had been previously accepted as self-evident. Descartes sought by this means to arrive at a more pure and intellectually honest position.

His work is quite profound and his method was revolutionary. While *Discourse on Method* was intended to be an honest assessment of truth, *by* questioning the self-evident existence of realities external to the mind, Descartes inadvertently gave birth to the idea that such realities were not a reliable indicator of truth.

These ideas set the stage for secular humanism, a complex philosophy that recognized rationality as the means to gain truth, but did not find sources of truth external to the human mind and spirit. It was marked by an increased optimism regarding the human race. Christian tradition had always regarded humanity as good but fallen and, therefore, in need of redemption. Secular humanists, however, either regarded humanity as "unfallen" (cf. Jean-Jacques Rousseau) or, if fallen, as its own savior. They believed that utopia could be achieved in this world through social systems, governments, and education. Contrary to these expectations, the modern era was marked by violent revolutions, increased desperation brought on by industrialization, and some of the deadliest wars in all of human history.

As a result of the perceived failure of secular humanism, some people grew skeptical of humanity's ability to solve its own problems, and so they grew skeptical of authority and social constructs. Not only was religious authority suspect, but governments and schools and "anyone over thirty" was a part of the problem. Tradition became synonymous with ignorance. In the arts, media, schools, and culture at large, truth was not something that was discovered outside of oneself. A person did not need to look to external reality for truth, as had the ancients, or to secular humanism, as had the moderns; instead, one only had to look "inside."

This way of thinking ushered in the postmodern era. In the postmodern world, humanity discovered that it had the potential to be so incredibly wrong that it could destroy itself. Therefore, it was thought that even humanity was not a reliable source of truth. If descriptions of reality (whether merely philosophical or theological) were not the source of truth, and humanity had been demonstrated to be a limited source of truth, then where could one look for "truth"? It would seem that the only credible source of truth would be in the individual or the subjective self. One consequence of this way of thinking is that ideas became virtually inseparable from the individual. If I am the source of truth, then "my truth" is just as legitimate as "your truth." In addition, if one criticizes "my truth," they criticize *me*.

Can we recover objective truth?

CHAPTER FOUR

The T-Word

Thanks to the Internet, we live in an "information age," where information is easily accessible. There are good things and bad things about this. The good thing is the accessibility of information; the bad thing is the quality of information available. Of course, there is some very good information available—I won't deny that—but much of it consists of opinions and not necessarily educated or informed ones. A seemingly infinite number of bloggers are all trying to push their opinions on others. This can be annoying at times, but it's not the real problem. The real problem is that people who are exposed only to opinions start to believe that the only thing that exists is opinion. And so they begin to believe that reality and belief are mere opinions.

The result is that we do not so much live in an "information age" as in an "opinion age."

But are all beliefs mere opinions? Or is there such a thing as truth? These become the questions people ask themselves. Now, as a Catholic, I believe truth exists, but, obviously, that doesn't mean others likewise believe truth exists. I want others to know truth exists, but before I can prove that, I must define it.

What Is Truth?

Truth can be defined pretty simply: it is the expression of *what is*. Therefore, the validity of a statement depends upon its conformity to what is. For example, if I were to say, "There is a computer on my desk," the statement would be true because it conforms to what *is*. There *is* a computer on my desk. Also, if I were to say that a computer, a scanner, and a fan are on my desk (and they are), the statement would reflect reality in even more detail.

Let's take the next step. There are also two kinds of truth: subjective truth and objective truth. Subjective truth is easily seen in the following sentences: "I like the summertime." "I like driving a bit over the speed limit." "I like Caribou Coffee." "I get sleepy after two glasses of wine."

Can you see the common factor among all the statements above? It's the *subject* of the statement; they all share the same subject—I. People of the opinion age believe that there are only "I" statements—opinion statements. And yet we know that there's more. We know that if there was only subjective truth, whenever people disagreed, there would only be three ways the disagreement could be resolved.

Might makes right. You disagree with me? I punch you in the face. If I can beat you up, I win.

The mob mentality. The majority decides what's right. If you disagree, I still might be able to punch you in the face, but that won't be as effective as a poll. The best way to see who's right is to see how many people agree with my opinion. If I can get more people to agree with my opinion than you can, then I'm right.

But we should realize that truth cannot be determined by the mob or the majority because truth is independent of these things. For example, in Nazi Germany, the majority might have believed that Jewish lives did not matter. A consensus or majority doesn't make something true.

Agree to disagree. The argument could end with the all too common response, "Listen. You have your truth, and I have mine. You go live your life, and I will go live mine." Now this might avoid conflict, but it also contributes to the growing inability of people to talk seriously to one another about important matters about which they disagree. In turn, that inability contributes to greater fragmentation of our society into small, isolated groups of people defined by unassailable views, with no way to resolve their differences. Without the common recognition of objective truth and our ability to know the truth of things, community tends to dissolve. Objective truth is easily seen in the following sentences: "Summers in Minnesota have an average high temperature of eighty degrees." "You can get a large Caribou Coffee for $1.89." "The speed limit outside my house is thirty miles an hour."

Those statements are all about the object; they conform to something outside of the subject. Because of this, people can argue about them. For example, one might observe that the speed limit posted outside my house is not what I claim it to be, saying, "Oh no, the speed limit outside your house is actually thirty-five miles per hour." The person making this observation could do so without attacking me because the object is outside of me. This truth, which conforms to reality, can now be demonstrated, proving that my earlier statement was not true.

Because objective truth exists outside of me, a thing can be true or false *regardless* of whether I know it, like it, or believe it. For example, at the University of Minnesota Duluth, where I work, virtually the entire campus is connected by a system of tunnels. Therefore, a student could feasibly spend the entire school year inside. (This does happen, believe it or not.) It might be storming or sunny outside, but these students wouldn't know it. Does the student's knowledge of the weather outside affect it? Does his wish for beautiful weather make it so? If he believes it to be sunny, is it actually so? The answer is no to all these questions. If it's storming outside, it's an objective fact, and someone's knowledge, desire, or belief cannot change that.

Regarding objective and subjective statements, a professor at the University of Minnesota Duluth tried to help his students understand that these are not the same things. In class, he would project different statements onto the screen, and the students were supposed to identify whether the statements were objective or subjective. With each slide, the students would cry out either "That's objective!" or "That's subjective!" This went on for a while until the class came to the following statement: "God exists." At that moment, there was near universal breakdown. The class ceased giving the same answer in unison; instead, there were two answers being shouted. Some students recognized right away that the statement was objective, but the majority of them thought the statement was subjective. (Remember that the professor wasn't claiming that the statement was objectively *true*; he was merely claiming that it was an objective statement.) One reason many students gave for saying the statement was subjective was that they had been raised in a culture where statements like "God doesn't exist" and "God exists" are regarded as simply matters of opinion.

The Principle of Noncontradiction

So truth concerns *what is*, and truth can be either subjective or objective. The principle of noncontradiction states that a thing cannot both *be* and *not be* at the same time and in the same way. For example, if there are eight chairs in a room, there cannot, at the same time, be zero chairs in the room.

Here is a quick story that deals with the noncontradiction principle. I have the opportunity to do a lot of marriage prep with couples on campus. A number of years ago, I worked with an interesting couple. The bride-to-be was a practicing Catholic, while the groom-to-be was an atheist. I knew this difference of belief could cause problems in their future, so I knew I had to bring it up. I kept trying to hint at it throughout marriage prep (I *am* from Minnesota after all, and we specialize in avoiding conflict), but eventually I was forced to address it point-blank.

"Okay. So you believe in God, and you're Catholic," I said to the bride-to-be. Next, I addressed her fiancé, saying, "And you do not believe in God, and you have left the Catholic Church." I turned back to the bride-to-be and asked, "Do you understand that you are about to marry and covenant your life to someone who believes you are 100 percent wrong when it comes to the *biggest* question in life?" This got her thinking.

I said the same thing to her future husband.

What was most interesting to me about our conversation was the man's response. He looked at me, and with complete sincerity, said, "Well, I don't believe that's the most important question in life." This got *me* thinking. If we consider God's existence to be simply a subjective kind of thing—believing that God exists is nice if it helps you sleep at night, it's nice if it gives you some comfort, it's nice if it gives you a sense of meaning or purpose—then it doesn't *really* make a difference.

But does it make a difference? What are the ramifications of God's not existing? I can think of three. We spoke of these briefly in chapter one when we discussed the atheist worldview. Let's take another and deeper look at them.

Consequence 1:

If God does not exist, there is no free will.

If God does not exist, then all of human thought and choice is completely material. Human beings are simply chemical reactions, and consciousness is nothing more than an illusion; choice is simply a result of cause and effect.

If human beings don't have free will, then we are just highly complex machines that respond to external and internal stimuli. If you put a dollar in a vending machine and you press the button but nothing comes out, you don't stand there and engage the machine in a discussion, saying, "Now see here, vending machine, the arrangement was I give you a dollar, I press the button, and you give me a soda." That's silly. Instead, you kick it! You shake it! Why? Because the vending machine didn't *decide* it was not going to give you a soda; it is simply not doing what you want it to do. So you might as well use force to get it to do what you want.

Man cannot have dignity if he does not have free will. There would be no essential uniqueness to any individual. He would simply *exist*. He might exist on a more complicated plane than inanimate matter, but he wouldn't exist on a more valuable plane.

Consequence 2:

If God does not exist, there is no right or wrong.

"Can a person be good without believing in God?" As we noted earlier, the most obvious and sensible response to this common question is, "Of course."

But the question isn't "Can you be good without *believing in God?*" The real question is "Can you be good if God doesn't exist?" And the answer is no. If God doesn't exist, then the universe is an accident. If the universe is an accident, then there is no such thing as right or wrong. If there is no such thing as right or wrong, nothing you do deserves praise or blame. The only thing driving your choice is utility or preference.

If there is no God, there are still things we like or don't like and things we prefer or don't prefer. There are also things that are either helpful or not for the growth of our species and its preservation. But without God in the picture, neither the existence of life nor its preservation is a good; instead, it's simply what I prefer or think useful. Then the question arises: "Useful for what?" Useful for a moral life? But is there any possible moral demand in life if the whole thing is an accident? This brings us to the third consequence.

Consequence 3:

If God does not exist, there is no meaning in the universe.

A number of years ago, I met with some FOCUS (Fellowship of Catholic University Students) missionaries in North Carolina. As a team-bonding exercise, we went out to walk around an art gallery. It was fascinating, but the entire gallery was filled with postmodern art (the kind of art where there is a toilet in one corner and an unmade bed in another). On one of the walls, there was a certain painting that caught my attention. It was huge, something like ten feet by ten feet, and was painted entirely red with two or three little dark smudges. I must have stood there for fifteen minutes just looking at it, taking it all in. It was big, and it was red, and I was just struck by it.

As I stood there, I must have looked like I knew what I was doing because two men walked up next to me, looked at me, looked at the painting, and then looked at me again and politely asked, "Excuse us, but what do you see?"

I am not kidding you, for the next fifteen minutes I described the *color red*: "I think it's this; this stuff here represents this; the red itself is meant to indicate this other thing"; and so forth. In total, I looked at this painting for thirty minutes. (That's thirty minutes of my life I will never get back.)

I spent half an hour observing and describing what the painting meant to *me*, not what the painting meant in and of itself. If I wanted to know what the painting *really* meant, whom would I have to ask? The artist, of course. Now, let's say the artist walked in the room while I was admiring her painting, and I told her, "Here's what I think your painting means." And the painter responded, "Well, that's a funny interpretation of my painting. I was getting ready to paint so I stretched out this huge canvas on the floor. Then my cats walked by and knocked over all this red paint, which completely covered my canvas. Not knowing what to do with it, I hung it up and it dripped and dried this way. When I looked at it again, those couple of smudges, the size, and color all really struck me, so I decided to hang it up as art."

Now, what the artist would be saying is that the painting in and of itself doesn't mean anything; it was the result of an accident. I might find meaning in the painting, but the painting in and of itself—despite my finding meaning in it—is meaningless.

In a similar way, without God, the universe is an accident. Accidents, in and of themselves, don't have meaning. I could attempt to read meaning into it, saying, "There's meaning in the beauty of the sunset.... There's meaning in the beauty of a newborn baby…meaning in life that exists and continues to perpetuate." I also might find meaning in other things: in relationships, in my job, in my life, or in my children. But ultimately, if creation is an accident, then there is no real meaning. For the atheist, there can be no objective meaning *in anything* because it's all an accident.

So there are three consequences of God's not existing: there is no free will, there is no right or wrong, and there is no meaning to anything at all. And yet most of us would say that this does not describe our experience.

First, our experience tends to be that even though we don't always choose what we want or what we ought, we still recognize that we have a choice. We all behave as if there is such a thing as free will.

Second, while we might not always agree on the specifics of what's right or wrong, most of us, when pushed, will acknowledge that there are some things that are always right and some things that are always wrong. Previously, we saw that increasingly a large number of people sometimes talk as if they think there is no right and no wrong. Yet as I also noted most people would admit things such as rape and racism—or to push the matter further, slavery—are wrong.

Third, it's true that it can often be difficult to make sense out of many things in our lives. But though we may be unable to perceive clearly what it all means, we still have the sense that the universe has meaning. If we didn't, then we wouldn't experience seemingly meaningless things. We can do so only because we have some sense that this or that apparently meaningless thing contradicts how things ought to be. As C. S. Lewis noted, just as the notion of blindness would be meaningless in a universe without vision, so too the idea of meaninglessness wouldn't make sense to us unless we had some sense of meaning, however limited or partial that may be. Therefore, virtually everything in our experience points to reality, objective truth, and God's existence.

So there are good reasons to think, as Christians do, that God is real. If God exists, what does that mean for humanity? What does his existence have to do with the topic of this book? What does this have to do with sex?

CHAPTER FIVE

Good but Fallen

Years ago, when I was a young priest in Hibbing, Minnesota, I remember visiting a ninety-year-old woman in the hospital. Her children and her grandchildren surrounded her. At one point, one of her family members mentioned that one of the granddaughters was living with her boyfriend. I responded by saying, "I am sorry to hear that." The old woman then looked at me and said, "Well, what can you do? It's always been this way." She was referring to the fact that people have always been inclined to do their own thing and that they have always struggled with purity outside and inside of marriage.

There was definitely some truth to the old woman's generalization, enough to get me thinking: Has it always been this way? Have we always been inclined to do our own thing, go our own way? Luckily for us, Pope Saint John Paul II spent every Wednesday for five years essentially answering this question. Those Wednesday Audiences were later compiled and expounded upon in what some consider his greatest work, *The Theology of the Body*, which deals with subjects such as human relationships, human dignity, and human love.

He began the entire series with Matthew 19:7–9, a passage in which Jesus is questioned about his views on divorce and remarriage.

> They [some Pharisees] said to him, "Why then did Moses command one to give a certificate of divorce, and to put her away?" He said to them, "For your hardness of heart Moses allowed you to divorce your wives, *but from the beginning it was not so*. And I say to you: whoever divorces his wife, except for unchastity, and marries another, commits adultery; and he who marries a divorced woman, commits adultery." (emphasis added)

In this passage, the Pharisees challenge Jesus' teachings, citing how Moses allowed for divorce. Jesus refutes their challenge, explaining that Moses allowed for divorce because of the hardness of the people's hearts. Jesus then goes on to reveal that this hardness of heart was not always the case: "From the beginning it was not so." John Paul II launched his investigation into what it was like "from the beginning" with this Scripture passage, essentially asking the following questions: What was human experience from the beginning? What was our experience of ourselves? What was our experience of the other? What was our experience of God? What was our experience of love? In order to answer these deep questions and help reveal who we really are, John Paul II turned to the first couple of chapters of Genesis.

What he found—and what many of us naturally intuit—is that things now are not as they have always been. Things are not as they should be. Many people sense that something is off with our world. Whenever I talk with groups of high school or college students, they communicate this feeling, which comes from a combination of the evident injustice and suffering in the world around us and the personal brokenness of our own lives. We can see patterns of brokenness in the world, and we all experience some element of brokenness in our relationships with our parents or friends, or even within ourselves. Given this, we question the status quo: Is this how it is supposed to be? Was the world meant to be so imperfect? Were we meant to experience pain and betrayal and struggle? Was this God's intention in creating us?

Jesus answers our questions with a resounding no, essentially saying, "No, from the beginning it wasn't like this. From the beginning it was different."

So what was it like in the beginning? The Book of Genesis holds the answer to our question. In the Garden of Eden, Adam and Eve didn't experience the same kinds of alienation that we experience in our relationships. Scripture tells us that "the man and his wife were both naked, and were not ashamed" (2:25). This means that Adam and Eve were able to stand in front of each other naked, without a desire to cover themselves or be "on guard." Their relationship was full, complete, unbroken.

In addition to the harmony experienced between man and woman, they also experienced complete harmony in their relationship with God and with all of creation (cf. *Catechism of the Catholic Church*, no. 376). Even Adam's and Eve's deepest identity, their very selves, were integrated. They were not at war within themselves; instead, they experienced an inner unity and wholeness.

So what happened? What caused things to change?

Something Other Than God

At some point, something alien to God's original purpose entered the world; we call it sin. Judeo-Christian tradition teaches us that our first parents used their intellect and their will to *choose* something other than God, something other than genuine freedom and love.

The result of this abuse of freedom was fracturing and division in our human relationships. Not only was our relationship with God fractured, but so were our relationships with other people and our inner selves. Saint Paul's words perfectly capture our broken nature: "I am carnal, sold under sin. I do not understand my own actions. For I do not do what I want, but I do the very thing I hate" (Rom 7:14–15). He is pointing out the internal brokenness we all share. Though we are made for greatness, we struggle to be great because we are still fallen. Seventeenth-century philosopher and mathematician Blaise Pascal explains how man is uniquely conscious of his own brokenness, saying, "The greatness of man is great in that he knows himself to be miserable. A tree does not know itself to be miserable."[1]

Legends of the Fall

What are the consequences of the Fall other than fractured relationships? How does it affect us as individuals? We've noted that to be human is to be both a soul and a body. Like the angels, we have minds and wills, qualities of our souls. Like other animals, we have emotions and senses, qualities of our bodies. The Fall has left wounds in us that touch both body and soul. Catholic tradition has pointed out three. The first is the darkening of our intellect, meaning that our minds, made to grasp truth, have a harder time perceiving what is true with clarity and consistency as before the Fall. We are liable to be caught by deception and illusion about ourselves, others, and the world.

The second consequence deals with the will. Our wills, made to reach out toward what is good, have lost strength in acting for the good. I can know what I ought to do but often fail to do it. For example, on many occasions I have tried to go on a diet.

---

[1] Blaise Pascal, *Pensées* 6.397, trans. W. F. Trotter, in *The Harvard Classics*, vol. 48, *Blaise Pascal: Thoughts, Letters, and Minor Works*, ed. Charles William Eliot (New York: P. F. Collier & Son, 1910).

I know that it would be beneficial for me, and I'm committed to doing it—at least in the beginning. But when the third day of my diet comes around, a doughnut sounds more delicious than ever. The next thing I know, I'm sitting down on the couch with an empty box of doughnuts lying open next to me. More seriously, I know that I shouldn't lie, or speak negatively about others, or act selfishly to get whatever I can for myself. I know I shouldn't act out of pride or envy or cowardice. And I want to do what's right in all those areas. Mostly. But often enough I fail through weakness of will.

The third consequence of the Fall involves emotions and sensual desires. We were made to live in harmony with ourselves: our minds were to point out what was true, our wills would move toward and act on what was good, and our emotions and physical desires would naturally come into line with goodness and truth and support us in them. But with the Fall, as our minds and wills threw off the rule of God, so our bodily nature was afflicted with a tendency to rise against our reason, and to push against our wills, and to be attracted to what would lead neither to truth nor to love.

All of these wounds have not taken from us the image of God. We are still created for goodness, and we still possess the dignity that comes from being God's children. But we have certainly fallen, and we've got a fight on our hands to regain our inner harmony.

Truth and Consequences

In 2011 Lady Gaga came out with the song "Born This Way." One of the verses is as follows:

> I'm beautiful in my way
> 'Cause God makes no mistakes. I'm on the right track, baby
> I was born this way.

Lady Gaga made no bones about what she was trying to say with these lyrics. Around the world, many people who had previously felt uncomfortable with the experience of their sexuality embraced this song as a triumphant anthem.

Although we are good, and although it is good we exist, we need to remember we are all fallen. This means that, while "God don't make junk," a consequence of the Fall is that we are *not*, in fact, perfect. So not everything we desire is good for us.

I have heard many people defend their behavior, saying, "Well, it can't be bad because God made me this way." The rationalization is that whatever sin they commit is not their fault because God gave them the attraction to this or that particular sin. I most often hear this argument when people are talking about their sexual attraction, whether their desires are homosexual or heterosexual. If we take this argument to its logical conclusion, the deficiency becomes obvious. For example, one could just as easily say, "God gave me this nasty temper," or, "God made me with this cocky attitude," or, "God just made me super talkative, so I have to gossip." (Believe it or not, I have actually heard people make this last excuse.) What one is ultimately claiming is that everything one does is somehow God's fault—but is this really true? If it were, we would be no more than programmed robots because we wouldn't be responsible for anything we do. When we start assigning blame to God, we have made a serious misstep: first, because it gets God wrong; and second, because it gets us wrong.

God never causes anyone to be tempted. In the Letter of James, the author goes to some length to clarify this truth. He writes, "Let no one say when he is tempted, 'I am tempted by God'; for God cannot be tempted with evil and he himself tempts no one" (1:13). Simply because a person feels this or that attraction does not imply that God approves of this attraction. To say this would not only be a misunderstanding of who God is, but a misunderstanding of human nature. James goes on to say, "Each person is tempted when he is lured and enticed by his own desire" (1:14).

As a side point, one positive aspect of these excuses is that the people who use them recognize the existence within themselves of an attraction toward something sinful. There can be no progress in the spiritual life until we acknowledge the reality of our present circumstances. So, if I happen to struggle with something, it is better to admit it than hide it. Sometimes we can be so shocked by our sins that we would rather ignore them or pretend they don't hurt us than bring them to the love and mercy of Jesus.

Catholic Christians believe that God made us good. We are created in his image and likeness, and we will bear that image and likeness into eternity. But, while we retain that intrinsic human goodness and dignity, not everything in us is good.

When we experience an attraction to sin, the last thing we should do is believe the lie that "God made me this way." Jesus Christ came to this earth to suffer, die, and rise from the dead. Why? For our redemption. That's why he sent the Holy Spirit. That's why he gave us the Church. God's plan is to save and redeem us from the wounded desires that can so often dominate our lives and to do so by "remaking" us according to his will.

While we strive to allow God to heal our "original wound," as Father Benedict Groeschel calls Original Sin,[2] we must

---

[2] Benedict J. Groeschel, CFR, *Healing the Original Wound: Reflections on the Full Meaning of Salvation* (Ann Arbor, MI: Servant Publications, 1993).

understand that this often takes time and that it can also be painful and difficult. This is an invitation to be patient with yourself in your wounds and to be patient with the people around you in their wounds. It is an invitation to continue to teach the truth: God has more than this or that attraction or desire in store for you. His plan for your life is freedom. His plan for your life is redemption. His plan for your life is *love*.

CHAPTER SIX

Made for Love

Man cannot live without love. He remains a being that is incomprehensible for himself, his life is senseless, if love is not revealed to him, if he does not encounter love, if he does not experience it and make it his own, if he does not participate intimately in it.

—Pope Saint John Paul the Great[*]

On December 14, 2004, I received a Facebook message from an old college friend. More specifically, it was from the woman who, at one point, I thought I would marry. I can remember the day our relationship ended as if it happened last week. At the time, I was a missionary in Central America, and letters were the best way for us to communicate. We had been sending about two letters a day to each other the entire time I was there. But as the weeks passed, it had become clearer and clearer that God was calling me to enter the seminary once I returned to the United States.

---

[*] John Paul II, encyclical *Redemptor Hominis* (March 4, 1979), no. 10, http://w2.vatican.va/content/john-paul-ii/en/encyclicals/documents/hf_jp-ii_enc_04031979_redemptor-hominis.html.

This woman is incredibly gifted and intelligent. She knew something was going on and realized that we needed to have a "real" conversation—a conversation over the phone. I agreed, so we arranged for her to call me on the only phone I had access to, located in the village nearby.

That Friday night, at seven o'clock, I found myself sitting in the dark, waiting for the phone to ring. Finally, it rang, and I quickly picked it up. "Hi, Mel." "Hi," she responded and paused briefly before continuing. "So, what's going on?" "Um—I think... I think that I need to go to the seminary next year." Tears were streaming down my face. Silence. After a brief moment, this incredible woman said, "Well, I knew that this was a possibility before we started dating."

Wow, what a thoughtful response. I couldn't believe it. She was just so selfless. I felt terrible and wished I could stay with her; but I also knew that I needed to at least *try* the seminary. Heartbroken and deeply saddened, I said, "I'm so sorry, Mel. I'm just so sorry."

"I know," she immediately responded. "But if this is what God wants for your life, then this is what he wants for my life too. If God is calling you somewhere else, that means he is calling me somewhere else as well."

I was stunned. Her generosity and insight moved me. This woman had always been one of the most caring and sensitive people I had ever known, and this was abundantly evident at the end of our relationship. Mel probably knew she could have talked me out of going to seminary, but she refrained from doing so. If she had chosen to do so, it wouldn't have been much of a fight. I think she knew that too. I was just *so* in love with her that I might have given in immediately.

Though I hadn't seen Mel for years, I saw the same caring and sensitive person in the Facebook message she sent me on December 14, 2004. Mel had been working in the Pacific Northwest for an organization that helped young men and boys, runaways who were living on the streets. Her work consisted of taking them in, listening to them, and caring for them. Many of these boys ran away from home because they experienced rejection or abuse from their families. She wrote to me that a common reason these boys were rejected was that they experienced same-sex attractions or confusion about their sexual identity.

Her message read, "I'm just so angry at the Church. I can't believe in an institution that would tell these boys (who had been so rejected by the ones who were supposed to love them) that they are *wrong* or *broken*."

I could hear Mel's generous and loving heart beat throughout the entire message. It was the same heart that noticed others, that felt the pain of others, and that had eventually led her to Portland to care for homeless youth.

I understood her frustration, although I did not agree with her claim regarding the Church. Clearly, the parents and guardians who were supposed to care for these young men failed to do so. Instead of feeling safe within their families, these young men experienced the pain of rejection and, sometimes, violence because they identified as gay. And that was not right. This *is* not right. These boys were not given a place of refuge; instead, they were driven from their homes and families simply because they identified as gay.

That is not right. That is not love. And that is not the message of the Church.

What Is Love, Anyway?

The quotation at the beginning of this chapter by Pope Saint John Paul II states that a human being cannot live without love. Every human being—regardless of sexual orientation, regardless of past experiences of relationship, regardless of how he may have been treated by family members—is made for love. Every person is intended by God to be loved. There is no one who is excluded from this.

But what is love? Of course, love is often a feeling—a feeling of affection we have for other people. But love is more than a noun; it's also a verb—an action, not just an emotion. We clearly need a good working definition of love. Luckily, a thirteenth-century Dominican friar named Saint Thomas Aquinas gave us this definition of love: "To love is to wish good to someone."[1] Saint Thomas knew that love often involves emotion, but, more importantly, he knew love must also be effective (doing) rather than merely affective (feeling).

"He who loves another looks upon his friend as another self, he counts his friend's hurt as his own, so that he grieves for his friend's hurt as though he were hurt himself."[2] This is affective mercy or love, in which one's heart is moved by the pain of another. The person's pity is rooted in "affection."

Of course, this is a good thing. Affection drives us on to love. The emotion that we get from love is good. Emotion, in and of itself, is not a bad thing! In fact, it is this very emotion, this very desire, that often moves us out of ourselves. Yet mere emotion is not enough. When Saint Thomas referred love to counting a friend's troubles as one's own, he meant much more than *feeling* bad along with a friend.

---

[1]   *The Summa Theologiæ of St. Thomas Aquinas* I-II, 26, 4, trans. Fathers of the English Dominican Province, second and revised ed., 1920, NewAdvent.org, online edition by Kevin Knight, 2017.

[2]   Ibid., II-II, 30, 2.

More Than a Feeling

A number of years ago, Steve Carell starred in the movie *Dan in Real Life*. In the movie, Carell's character, Dan Burns, is a father of three young girls. His middle daughter, a high school student, has a boyfriend. At one point in the movie, Carell—who is going through his own moment of infatuation with his brother's girlfriend—sits down to speak with his daughter's boyfriend about their relationship. As the adult, he assumes the role of "teacher." But, surprisingly, by the end of the conversation, it appears that the role has been reversed. He has become the one who needs to be taught, and the young man has become the teacher. The boyfriend's words of advice to him are: "Mr. Burns, love isn't a feeling.... It's an *ability*."

"Love isn't a feeling.... It's an ability." I am sure that you have heard that idea (or a similar idea) hundreds of times. But what does it mean?

First, it means what was said above: love is not merely an affective emotion; it must be an effective choice. If love is an ability, then loving is something that a person can be either very good at or very bad at. If love is an ability, one needs to *learn* how to do it. I can't merely rely upon my instincts or passions to direct my actions; I need to train myself to love well.

Dr. Edward Sri, a professor at the Augustine Institute in Denver, Colorado, once visited our campus in Duluth to give a talk on love and relationships. He pointed out that mere emotion or passion for a thing or person can never guarantee proficiency. Dr. Sri used flying to illustrate his point.

"Imagine that you are passionate about flying airplanes. Whenever you see an airplane, your heart begins to race. Whenever you drive by the airport, you always strain your neck to see if you can catch a glimpse of a plane taking off or landing. You are so passionate about airplanes that you have posters of different airplanes all over your room; and anytime someone mentions flying, you are not able to concentrate on anything else. If this was you, a person could reasonably say that you were 'passionate' about flying."

"But," he asked, "would that passion *qualify* you to pilot a plane? To put it another way, would you be willing to get in a plane that was piloted by someone who is *passionate* about flying, but has never been *trained* to fly?"

Obviously, you would never trust someone to fly a plane simply because that person had a passion for flying. You would, however, be willing to get in an airplane and trust your life to someone who was *both* passionate about flying and a trained pilot. You likely would even be willing to trust someone who wasn't passionate about flying but who was a great pilot. But a sane person would only trust someone who developed the *ability* to fly well.

In the same way, it would be unwise to entrust your heart to someone who was passionate about love and about *you*, if that person didn't possess the *ability* to love. Being passionate about a person and having strong feelings for him does not guarantee that you will love that person well. We are made for love, but we are also wounded by excessive self-love. Love is what you have been "born to do," and yet no one is born with the ability to do this well. We must *learn* how to love well. And doing so is not only a matter of taking in more information, but also a matter of *transformation*.

God Is Love

Pope Benedict pointed this out in his very first encyclical, *Deus Caritas Est* (God Is Love). In the first paragraphs, he noted that there are some in history who would criticize

Christianity for "poisoning" romantic love.[3] Pope Benedict specifically mentions that Friedrich Nietzsche complained that Christianity degenerated erotic love into a vice. In contrast to other civilizations or philosophies that exalted love (like the ancient Greeks), Nietzsche claimed that Christianity made love into something evil.[4]

And yet, Pope Benedict noted:

> Let us take a look at the pre-Christian world. The Greeks—not unlike other cultures—considered *eros* principally as a kind of intoxication, the overpowering of reason by a "divine madness" which tears man away from his finite existence and enables him, in the very process of being overwhelmed by divine power, to experience supreme happiness. All other powers in heaven and on earth thus appear secondary: *"Omnia vincit amor"* says Virgil in the *Bucolics*—love conquers all—and he adds: *"et nos cedamus amori"*—let us, too, yield to love (*Jenseits von Gut und Böse* X, 69). In the religions, this attitude found expression in fertility cults, part of which was the "sacred" prostitution which flourished in many temples.[5]

Therefore, while there were some people who seemed to treat *eros* as liberating and empowering and who "yielded" themselves to it, this was at the cost of others. Their surrender to love (as they understood it) involved not what was not really an ascent to greatness, whatever they thought was the case, but a descent to selfish use.

Pope Benedict continues:

---

[3] Benedict XVI, encyclical letter *Deus Caritas Est* (December 25, 2005), nos. 1–4, esp. no. 5, http://w2.vatican.va/content/benedict-xvi/en/encyclicals/documents/hf_ben-xvi_enc_20051225_deus-caritas-est.html.

[4] Cf. *Jenseits von Gut und Böse* 4.168.

[5] *Deus Caritas Est*, no. 4.

The Old Testament firmly opposed this form of religion, which represents a powerful temptation against monotheistic faith, combating it as a perversion of religiosity. But it in no way rejected *eros* as such; rather, it declared war on a warped and destructive form of it, because this counterfeit divinization of *eros* actually strips it of its dignity and dehumanizes it.... An intoxicated and undisciplined *eros*, then, is not an ascent in "ecstasy" towards the Divine, but a fall, a degradation of man. Evidently, *eros* needs to be disciplined and purified if it is to provide not just fleeting pleasure, but a certain foretaste of the pinnacle of our existence, of that beatitude for which our whole being yearns.[6]

In reminding his readers that love is not merely an instinct that one blindly follows, but is something that needs to be "disciplined and purified," Pope Benedict snaps us back to the reality of our broken condition as well as our need to develop the ability to love.

Transformation Involves Training

Clearly, the intellect is very important when it comes to being able to love well. If love is "willing the good of the other," then one's intellect has to be formed to know what "the good" truly is. But the will is just as important in developing the ability to love well. Often we know what is good, but, because of the Fall, fail to choose it. In most cases, our passions trump our will, and we find ourselves obeying our thirst.

Dan and Chip Heath commented on this phenomenon in their book *Switch*. In *Switch*, they attempt to explain why we so often fail to choose the good when we know we should. From a completely nonreligious point of view, the two authors recognize that the human intellect (the part of us that *knows*

---

[6]   Ibid.

good and evil) and the human will (the part of us that *chooses* good and evil) are often overwhelmed by the passions. Our passions are so powerful, in fact, that Dan and Chip describe them as the "elephant," while our intellect and will are merely the "rider" on the back of the elephant.[7] Most of the time, no matter how much the rider knows where he wants to go, the elephant seems to do its own thing.

People don't need a book, however, to tell them this. We all know it by experience. If you have ever tried to follow a diet or exercise regularly, you know how the "elephant" seems to be in control. Promising to love another person is no guarantee that you won't eventually fall in love with someone else. The heart wants what the heart wants—but just because you want something does not mean you ought to choose it.

Even the Bible talks about this deep pain of desiring something that we know isn't good for us or for another. As was noted earlier, Saint Paul wrote:

> I do not understand my own actions. For I do not do what I want, but I do the very thing I hate. Now if I do what I do not want, I agree that the law is good. So then it is no longer I that do it, but sin which dwells within me. For I know that nothing good dwells within me, that is, in my flesh. I can will what is right, but I cannot do it. For I do not do the good I want, but the evil I do not want is what I do. Now if I do what I do not want, it is no longer I that do it, but sin which dwells within me. So I find it to be a law that when I want to do right, evil lies close at hand. For I delight in the law of God, in my inmost self, but I see in my members another law at war with the law of my mind and making me captive to the law of sin which

---

[7] Chip Heath and Dan Heath, *Switch: How to Change Things When Change Is Hard* (New York: Crown Publishing Group, 2010).

dwells in my members. Wretched man that I am! Who will deliver me from this body of death? (Rom 7:15–24)

All of this is to say that our love—or our ability to love—is disordered. Our nature, created good, has been damaged. We are all, in various ways, "not quite right." We are disordered not only in *how* we love, but also in *what* we love. We oftentimes love the wrong things!

Out of Order

Home movies can be funny, but they can also be incredibly embarrassing for those who have a starring role in them. I was recently speaking with a friend named Whitney. She and her siblings are all grown and out of the house, and a few years ago, at Christmas time, her family sat down to watch some old home movies of past Christmases. Whitney was mortified. In the videos, she was, shall we say, not her best self. Racing from one present to another, she would open one to see what she had been given and would then discard it immediately so that she could open her next present. As she watched the video, everyone laughed at her antics, but Whitney looked at her parents and asked, "How was I such a greedy little kid? Why didn't you send me to my room or something?"

Whitney's experience should resonate with a lot of us. We have all been there. It might not have been a Christmas present, but it was certainly something similar. All of us have had to face the choice between letting go of a toy and keeping a friend, or not sharing a toy and losing a friend. We have all experienced a certain *disorder* in our desires.

When it comes to same-sex attractions, the Catholic Church explains it as a case where our affection, or our attractions, are disordered. Please don't misunderstand me. I am not saying that only homosexual attractions are disordered. When it comes to sexual desire, almost all of our passions get amplified. A heterosexual man desires to have sexual relations with someone who is not his wife. This is an example of the disordered affection. A homosexual man desires to look at gay porn. This is a disordered desire. A heterosexual woman gets lost or excessively involved in her romance novels. This is an example of loving the wrong thing. A homosexual woman longs to be sexually intimate with her closest friend. These are examples where what we want is, to different degrees and in varying respects, "off."

There Is Power Here

Affective love is powerful. It is that "good feeling" that we get when we love another person or another place or another thing. While this love is good, there also happens to be an even better, even more powerful kind of love. This love is called effective love, and it's a love that actually moves us, instead of simply being something warm we can rest in, like a warm blanket. True, affective love feels great, but effective love *moves*—it does something; it is love that goes out of the self. A love that can go out of the self is worth thinking about.

Love involves willing. To will something is to choose it. It is more than just wanting something; instead, it involves taking action based on a desire. I live in northern Minnesota, where many people have cabins. These cabins are used in the summer but remain unused in the winter. Imagine going up to one of these rustic cabins in the middle of January. If you entered the cabin, it would be absolutely freezing inside, almost as cold as it is outside. A person might walk into this cold cabin, sit at the kitchen table, and truly desire to be warm. Yet there is a difference between the person who is sitting there shivering, *wanting* to be warm, and the person who gets up, goes outside, gets the firewood, brings it inside, lights a fire in the fireplace, and *chooses* to make it warm.

This is the difference between wanting and willing. I notice that I would sometimes prefer to *want* to love another person rather than actually *choose* to love another person. I want to do the good. I want to love people. I must, however, recognize that there is a difference between my *wanting* someone else's good and my actually *willing* someone else's good. The first is affective and the second is effective. To will something is to choose to act. Therefore, to love someone touches on the action of love. I am going to *will* something; I am going to *choose* something; I am going to *do* something—which leads us to the second part.

Love is willing the good. What is someone's good? I mean, who is to say what the good of another is, anyway?

First, in order to know what is good for a thing, we have to know the nature of that thing. That is why we examined the nature of things in a previous chapter. Therefore, to know what is good for a human being, we have to know what the nature of a human being is. We defined a human being as a body-soul unity made in God's image and likeness—a unity made for greatness, made for joy, made for love, made for freedom, and made for life. Because of this, when I will another person's good, what I will must be consistent with those things.

I remember speaking with a young woman on campus whose name was Shelly. Shelly got caught up in the "hook-up culture": she had sexual encounters with guys regularly, almost every weekend. She was lonely, and she was looking for love. In the course of those weekends, Shelly seemed to feel less lonely, even if only for a moment. She then would tell herself the rest of the following week that she had had a good time, that she wasn't lonely, and that she was desired because this or that guy had shown her interest. She also assured herself that she could get another guy to show interest in her the next weekend.

I remember asking Shelly, "Do you realize that what you're doing isn't love? Do you realize that the things you do to feel less lonely are only exacerbating the deep and painful loneliness you actually feel?" I fear she never came to see what I was trying to show her. Loving other people is not just giving them what they want; it's giving them what's good for them. It's willing their good.

Love Is Willing the Good of the Other

Love is almost always outwardly focused. While people need to be able to accept and love themselves, they must not be *selfish*. Love is not just a feeling you get for yourself, or a thing that you will for yourself. Love moves beyond the self. A document from the Second Vatican Council stated, "Man, who is the only creature on earth which God willed for itself, cannot fully find himself except through a sincere gift of himself (cf. Luke 17:33)."[8] You cannot be a gift to another or others and simultaneously be inwardly directed; instead, you must look *out*. One of the major problems we have in our hearts is that we are looking out for *numero uno*; we are *self*-centered.

Selfishness is a part of our fallen, damaged human nature. We are made for love—to give love as well as to receive love. We are made to love God and others, but often choose a

---

[8] Vatican Council II, Pastoral Constitution on the Church in the Modern World *Gaudium et Spes* (December 7, 1965), no. 24, http://www.vatican.va/archive/hist_councils/ii_vatican_council/documents/vat-ii_cons_19651207_gaudium-et-spes_en.html.

cheap imitation, like loving the self. I want what I want when I want it. The solution to the problem of self-love is not a masochistic rejection of everything I desire. Rather, I must learn to become attentive to the needs of others; I must move from myself and focus on another. Love isn't about what I get; it's about what I will for another, the good that I can will for another. So how can I go outside of myself?

Let's look at the image of God, as Love, as a Trinity: Father, Son, and Holy Spirit. From all eternity, the Father pours himself out in love to the Son, who receives that love and pours himself out in love to the Father. The love poured out between them is so real and total that it brings about another Person: the Holy Spirit. The love shared between the Father and Son and Holy Spirit is outwardly focused. If this is what love *is*, then this is what every human was made for.

We are made in God's image, so we reflect something of the way God is. This means, among other things, you are meant to be a gift. You are meant to love and to be loved. But we are often confused about this. Our culture has taken this massive term—"love"—and reduced it. For the most part, it has been simply reduced to romantic love, which has been further reduced to sex. This causes people to misunderstand John Paul II when he says, "Man cannot live without love."[9] The modern hearer is tempted to interpret that to mean, "Man cannot live without sex." But we know this is not true. Even the ancient Greeks understood this wasn't true. Interestingly enough, while there is only one word for "love" in English, the Greeks had at least four: *storgē*, the love of affection; *eros*, the love of desire; *philia*, brotherly love or true friendship; and *agapē*, the self-emptying love.

---

[9] *Redemptor Hominis*, no. 10.

Storgē is the love that we mean when we say "I love my dog," "I love my home," or "I love what my house smells like when I come home for Thanksgiving break." It's a love of affection that virtually everyone experiences regularly. In C. S. Lewis' book *The Four Loves*, he describes *storgē* as the love that is naturally able to love the unlovable simply because of familiarity and affection.[10]

The second kind of love is *eros*, the love of desire. It's the kind of love we associate with romance. At its best, this kind of love causes an individual to go out of himself to renounce everything for the other person. At its worst, *eros* causes the individual to want to "possess" the other person. *Eros* can be powerful in creating life, but it can also be powerful in destroying life. This is one of the reasons that the Greeks respected *eros* but didn't consider it to be the highest form of love.

Eros is powerful because it has energy; it has the power to get a man to walk across the room to ask someone out. *Storgē*, however, is cozier; it's something you can nestle into without really acting on it. The former is largely effective, while the latter is largely affective.

Philia can be understood as the love between two true friends. It does not merely tolerate the presence of the other person, but truly enjoys his presence. Unlike *eros*, it doesn't think too often about the relationship in and of itself, and it is the least likely of the loves to lead to manipulation of the other. *Philia* is also quite rare. C. S. Lewis indicated that a person might experience *philia* only a small number of times in life. Since *philia* is so relatively rare, and because it is the least likely to be distorted, the Greeks considered it to be the highest form of love.

---

[10] C. S. Lewis, *The Four Loves* (New York: Mariner Books, 2012).

And yet, so many people still place a higher value on *eros* over *philia* when determining whom they love. I can't tell you how many married couples I have counseled where either the bride or the groom comes to me and says, "What do I do now? I just fell in love with someone who is not my spouse." I say, "Don't worry about it. That's just *eros*. You do not have to act on it."

Perhaps you don't agree with this high esteem for *philia* love. But consider this. Many young brides or grooms who come to me for premarriage counseling, in an attempt to indicate that their love is more special than other kinds of romantic love, will say, "I'm marrying my best friend." What they are really saying is that their love isn't just *eros*; it is something greater. That's wonderful. That's what we call *philia* love. These people are claiming that they have something greater than *eros*, and that's because they intuitively know that there is a love greater than *eros*! We truly long for *philia* love. Think about it: How many couples would rather be simply sexual partners than best friends with their spouses? Very few, and the few would do so to their own detriment.

When John Paul II pointed out that we could not live without love, he also stressed that we are made to be a self-gift, to be selfless: we are made for friendship. Every person, whether heterosexually oriented or homosexually oriented, is made for love—and is called to be a gift of love. This does not necessarily mean sex.

At World Youth Day 2004, Pope Saint John Paul II pointed out:

> It is not easy to forget our self, but if we do, it draws us away from possessive and narcissistic love and opens us up to the joy of a love that is self-giving. This Eucharistic school of freedom and charity teaches us to overcome superficial emotions in order to be rooted

firmly in what is true and good; it frees us from self-attachment in order to open ourselves to others. It teaches us to make the transition from an *affective* love to an *effective* love. For love is not merely a feeling; it is an act of will that consists of preferring, in a constant manner, the good of others to the good of oneself: "Greater love has no man than this, that a man lays down his life for his friends" (Jn 15:13).[11]

---

[11] Message of the Holy Father John Paul II to the Youth of the World on the Occasion of the XIX World Youth Day 2004 (February 22, 2004), no. 5 (emphasis in original), http://w2.vatican.va/content/john-paul-ii/en/messages/youth/documents/hf_jp-ii_mes_20040301_xix-world-youth-day.html.

CHAPTER SEVEN

Identity

On the evening of July 22, 1978, a fourteen-year-old girl named Jennifer found herself pinned against the ground by an unknown attacker. The man, twenty-four years old, had previously assaulted at least half a dozen other young women. He physically and sexually assaulted her. Immediately after, Jennifer called the police and dragged herself to a hospital. Several weeks later, Jennifer's baby bump clearly showed she was pregnant. Jennifer was terrified and wondered if she could bring a child of violence into a world like this.

Eight months and three days after the attack, Jennifer gave birth to a baby girl she named Melanie. Jennifer had just turned fifteen, and, knowing that she couldn't support her daughter, gave up Melanie for adoption. This baby, this "child of rape," was adopted by what seemed like a good family. But, tragically, in the third grade Melanie was abused by her uncle. The abuse continued until she was sixteen years old.

Hurt and ashamed, Melanie sought comfort in random sexual encounters. For the next several years, her life was a series of hookups. A fantastic athlete, she was able to get through college on athletic scholarships and outwardly seemed to have everything going for her. But internally it was different: Melanie felt like her entire life was marked. First, not only was she a child of rape, but she had also been abused as a child. Second, she was the kind of person who thought she deserved nothing more than abuse. Lastly, she was the kind of person who was abused not only by others, but also by herself.

Melanie experienced herself as broken, used, and unlovable. While she might have been outwardly successful, she did not see her life as having any kind of destination, any kind of real purpose. Then a great change came: someone stepped into Melanie's life when she was twenty-four years old and introduced her to Jesus Christ. Melanie's life was transformed. Melanie is now a religious sister who travels around the country speaking to young men and women about the truth of *their* origin, *their* story, and *their* destiny.

Many people ask themselves, "To what degree does my experience of my sexuality define me or give me my identity?" This question applies to all of us, including Sister Melanie. We all have an origin, a story, and a destiny, and how we look at these things determines how we perceive our identity.

Speaking of origins: I dated a girl during high school and into college for about three years. Her youngest brother is roughly seven years younger than she is. I distinctly remember the day when she looked at me sideways and said, "He was kind of an accident." Those words stuck with me; they rang out—even though I didn't say anything at the moment, I thought, "An accident? There's no such thing as an accident! No child is an accident!" I imagine that he grew up looking at himself as an accident and was influenced by this perception of his origin, thinking, "I was not wanted. I was not chosen. I am merely an accident."

This "origin story" can become even worse for a person whose beginning had been marked by violence. A child of rape might think, "Not only am I merely an accident, but I am the result of a violent action. What brought me into existence was violence, not love." This perception could be enough to give a person his identity, albeit a distorted one.

Ancestry.com is a website where anyone can track down ancestors. I have a number of friends who are interested in their genealogy. They want to know the story of their families and ancestors: what they did, how they lived, what kind of successes and failures they experienced. I understand this curiosity. One reason for tracking down our ancestors is the hope that we'll find something special, someone unique. In essence, we're hoping to find some greatness in our families. There is an unspoken belief that, if there is greatness in our families, then our origins (and identities) are great. That greatness is part of our personal stories; it's part of *who each of us is*—one's personal identity. "My great-great-grandmother helped slaves escape from the South." "My great-aunt saved lives during the Great Depression." "My grandfather knew General Patton." We would all like to "identify" with such ancestors. We are looking to give ourselves some kind of identity.

We can also see this phenomenon in the Bible. The Gospel of Matthew begins with the genealogy of Jesus. While we hear this genealogy every Advent, most people don't recognize the majority of the names, although we know some of them. Most of us are familiar with the stories of Adam, Abraham, Isaac, David, and Solomon. We might ask, "Why does Matthew start his Gospel with the genealogy of Jesus?" At first glance, we might suppose it was because the names listed represented heroes and great figures of Scripture. But if we were to dig a little deeper we would soon discover a different and in some ways a darker truth.

There are a number of people in the genealogy of Jesus who were decidedly not heroic. For example, there is Judah, who had a child by his daughter-in-law Tamar, thinking she was a prostitute. Jesus' ancestry runs through Tamar.

There is also the story of David, the king of Israel, whose son Solomon was famous for his wisdom. Solomon's mother, Bathsheba, became David's wife in terrible circumstances: after he had an affair with her that resulted in her becoming pregnant, David arranged for her husband, one of his soldiers, to be left alone in a battle so he would be killed by the enemy. David and Solomon are certainly ancestors of Jesus—Jesus is sometimes addressed as "the Son of David"—but David's bad behavior does not *define* Jesus.

People are often tempted to believe that they are an accident, that their origin is simply meaningless. And yet as Pope Benedict made very clear, "Each of us is the result of a thought of God. Each of us is willed, each of us is loved, each of us is necessary."[1] Pope Benedict is saying that despite the situations of your birth, or whatever you may have been told about your origin—that you were an accident, that you were a child of violence, that your life means nothing—your origin is the result of God's love. Your origin is love. Love is what gives you your identity.

"I'm the Goalie"

In addition to defining ourselves by origin, many of us are also tempted to define ourselves by our experiences. There was a man who had graduated from high school over thirty years ago. Upon meeting a former classmate, he re-introduced

---

[1] Homily of His Holiness Benedict XVI (St. Peter's Square, April 24, 2005), http://w2.vatican.va/content/benedict-xvi/en/homilies/2005/documents/hf_ben-xvi_hom_20050424_inizio-pontificato.html.

himself, saying, "I'm Jack. You remember me? I'm the goalie."
Now of course he was reminding his former classmate of how
he might remember him; but he didn't say, "I *was* the goalie";
he said, *"I'm* the goalie." In doing so, he allowed himself to be
defined by a position he played on their high school hockey
team thirty years prior.

The inclination to define ourselves by our story, our
experience, is very tempting for those who experience same-
sex attractions. For example, a person could say, "Well, I
experience an attraction to people of my sex. Therefore, I'm
gay. That is *who I am.* That is my identity." But while our
experiences are a *part* of our story, no experience is powerful
enough to give us our identity.

Years ago, I heard a talk given by Father John Harvey,
the founder of Courage (a Catholic organization dedicated
to helping men and women with same-sex attractions live
holy and happy lives), who described the following scenario:
Imagine a fifteen-year-old boy and his buddy behind a shed,
who out of curiosity smoked some cigarettes. If you busted
them, you probably wouldn't identify them as smokers.
But imagine the same fifteen-year-old boy going behind
the shed with the same buddy, but instead of smoking, they
experiment sexually with each other. Our culture responds
affirmatively, saying, "Oh! You've discovered you're gay.
That's *who you are.*" This is a completely different response
from the previous example. Why is that? Why are we so
quick to identity people by part of their story when the part is
related to their sexuality?

Now, I am not trying to minimize the potency of the
experience of sexuality; I'm just saying it doesn't give us our
identity. Clearly, being attracted to members of the same sex
is a more significant part of one's experience than being "the

goalie" or "smoking some cigarettes." But consider the case of Melanie. Her experience of abuse was deeply significant, and it had a powerful effect on her. But did her traumatic experience define her identity? She thought it did at one time; but she has found that she was mistaken. If Melanie's experience of sexuality didn't give her *her* identity, why would anyone else's experience of sexuality be enough to define them?

Even while I write these words, I know that I am over-looking the obvious. I am "straight." Because of that fact, I don't see myself as being unique. I am "on the inside" when it comes to my sexuality—part of the "majority." This colors my viewpoint. Let me share another story to illustrate this.

Each of us has a story, and each of us has many experiences. For Sister Melanie, part of her experience was her self-perception as someone who was used, someone who was worthless, and someone who had even hurt herself. Since that was part of her story, and a real part of her experience, it became what she came to regard as her identity. Our story and experiences can become the lens through which we see ourselves.

We are rarely accurate when we allow our experiences to define us. We can't help but define ourselves by our strengths and weaknesses: "I'm the goalie." "I'm smart." "I'm dumb." "I'm included." "I belong." "I'm shameful." "I'm used." "I'm unwanted." "I'm an addict." "I'm strong." "I'm weak." For those who succeed, who seem to thrive in our culture, there is a strong temptation to define themselves by their successes. And apparently this is also why people who are successful in one area of their life often consider themselves to be an expert in other areas, too.

Having a homosexual or heterosexual attraction might be part of your experience, and a significant part no doubt. But is this your identity? No. The truth revealed to us by Christ makes clear that your sexual orientation is not what ultimately defines you. If we allow ourselves to be defined by our sexual attractions, we are reducing ourselves and defining ourselves by something far too small.

You Have a Destiny

One last element that shapes your identity is your true *destiny*. Before the time of Christ, most people in the Greco-Roman world believed their ultimate destiny was simply to go to Hades and spend eternity there. For Jews influenced by Greek thought, Sheol was a similar concept; it was the abode of the dead. Still others might have believed that the self was annihilated at death. Yet Scripture reveals that our destiny is greater than this. We're made for more; we're made for love. Our destiny is life eternal with God in Heaven.

Everyone has a destiny, and this is not the same thing as fate. The difference between fate and destiny is that fate implies the absence of free will. If you are fated to do something or go somewhere, you have no control over what happens. Destiny, on the other hand, implies that you have a *destination*. Jesus has revealed to all of us that we have a destination, a reason for existence that goes beyond *this* existence, this life. Jesus further reveals that our destiny is love. Your destiny is to live forever in your Father's house.

Quoting the *Roman Catechism*, the *Catechism of the Catholic Church* puts it this way: " 'The whole concern of doctrine and its teaching must be directed to the love that never ends' (Preface 10)" (*CCC* 25). This is the primary reason for every doctrine that the Catholic Church proposes for belief: love. Continuing to quote the *Roman Catechism*, the *Catechism* states that " 'whether something is proposed for belief, for hope or for action, the love of our Lord must always be made accessible, so that anyone can see that all the works of perfect Christian virtue spring from love and have no other objective than to arrive at love.' "

This reminds me of one of my favorite stories in Scripture: the Parable of the Prodigal Son (Lk 15:11–32). We're all familiar with this story: A man has two sons. The younger son wants the inheritance that is coming to him (after the father dies—which is apparently too long for him to wait). The father gives it to him and he leaves home and spends all of his father's gift living unwisely. Then a famine strikes and the son doesn't have anywhere he can turn, so he starts working with pigs but is still starving.

The son—who comes from the father's home—has a purpose. However, he forgets his origin, and he forgets who he is. In fact, he is so far separated from his father's house, he is so far separated from his origin, and his story is so broken that he finds himself living in the midst of swine.

In Jewish culture there may have been no greater fall from grace. He finds himself not merely having betrayed his father, but having sinned and been separated completely from the community of Israel, living with pigs, one of the unclean animals. He was far from his father's house and far from everything connected to his father. In such a state, the young man seemed to say to himself, "This is who I am. My origin *used* to be my father's home, but no longer. I have disqualified myself. My story is broken and filled with wastefulness (prodigality) and foolishness. Look where I am! I am living in the midst of swine. There is no possible way that I can identify myself as a child of my father."

But what happens? The story goes that the young man comes to his senses. I remember reading a translation years ago that said, "Coming to himself," or, "Remembering himself" (cf. Lk 15:17). In this moment, when the young man was tempted to define himself wrongly by his story, he chooses instead to define himself differently, according to a truer measure: "Who am I really? I am not merely someone who left his father. I am not merely someone who finds himself stuck living with swine. I am made for more than this." Yet we know that his grip on his true identity is tenuous because he still sees himself as a slave. He says, "I will arise and go to my father, and I will say to him, 'Father, I have sinned against heaven and before you; I am no longer worthy to be called your son; treat me as one of your hired servants'" (Lk 15:18–19). He gets up, and he goes home.

You know how the story continues: "While he was yet at a distance, his father saw him and had compassion, and ran and embraced him and kissed him" (Lk 15:20). It's worth noting that in ancient Mediterranean culture, an elderly man would never run. He would have sat with noble dignity. It was a mark of respect from the younger to the older, and from sons to their fathers. He would have waited for his disgraced son to come before him. He would have sat, and the son would have respectfully stood. But here is the father, jumping up from his seat and racing to his son. And before the son can give his rehearsed speech asking for forgiveness, his father has already embraced him, called for the finest robe, a ring, and sandals to be given to the son. He then orders that the entire household feast on the fattened calf because "my son was dead, and is alive again; he was lost, and is found" (Lk 15:24).

Note the four things that he calls for: first, the finest robe; second, a ring on his finger; third, sandals for his feet; fourth, the fattened calf. All of these have meaning. The father didn't ask for just any robe to be placed on his filthy, stinking son. He asked for the *finest* robe. Why? Because the finest robe is worn by only the *favored* child, someone who is fully part of the family. He gives him a ring. What does the ring signify? The one who bears the ring is set apart as a member of the family and has the authority of the father. The father is sharing his authority with his lost son. Next, he gives his son sandals, shoes, as if to say, "If you want to leave again, you are free to go—not that I want you to go—but if you want to leave again, you are free to go. I will not stop you." Finally, there is the fattened calf, which explains itself. And then the celebration begins.

The son was tempted to define himself by misconduct, by the sum of his experience. But his father would not let him. As a result, he was not only received back into the family, but also restored to an even greater role in the household of his Father. We all have the same decision when we stray from Christ and the Church; the decision of whether or not we will "come to our senses (ourselves)," seek our true identity, turn our backs on false ones, and return to the Father's house, our true home. If you are someone who experiences same-sex attractions, the Father *desires* you to remember who you are.

You might think, "Well, maybe I'll be welcome in the Church," or, "Well, maybe . . . hopefully . . . I can have some sort of place at the table of the Lord." But when you come home, the Father always receives you and restores you to his family. When you come home, the Father welcomes you with great joy!

Years ago, I told Bishop Paul Sirba, my bishop, that I was giving a presentation on homosexuality in the Catholic Church. I asked him, "What should I say, Bishop?" He paused, then he looked at me and said, "I want every person who identifies as gay or lesbian in the Church to know how deeply loved they are. I want them to know that if I had a parish in my diocese that was filled *only* with gay and lesbian Catholics, I would love that parish so very much."

The lost son is welcomed home as a family member. This means that he *belongs*. He belongs in the family, in his Father's house. And if you have same-sex attractions, I have to make this absolutely clear: You are not merely welcomed in the Church; you *belong* in the Church. You are not merely welcomed back to the Father's house; you *belong* in the Father's house. You are not merely tolerated; you are loved.

God is the only reality "large" enough to give you a true identity. And God says that it is good that you exist. You are welcome in the Father's house. A difficult origin, a broken story, or a forgotten destiny are not enough to define your true identity. When we approach the Lord with our broken origins, stories, and destinies, he reveals and redeems our true origins, our actual stories, and our authentic destinies.

In 2002, Pope Saint John Paul II looked at me—and 1.5 million other Catholics—and said: "*We are not the sum of our weaknesses and failures*; we are the sum of the Father's love for us and our real capacity to become the image of his Son."[2]

"I am a gay Catholic man," you may say. Or, "I am a lesbian Catholic woman." You may think *that* is your story. But your identity is something else, something profound. You are a son or daughter of God. Your destiny is to live in him.

---

[2] Homily of the Holy Father John Paul II, 17th World Youth Day (Toronto, July 28, 2002), no. 5 (emphasis in original), https://w2.vatican.va/content/john-paul-ii/en/homilies/2002/documents/hf_jp-ii_hom_20020728_xvii-wyd.html.

CHAPTER EIGHT

What Are You Looking For?

It is Jesus in fact that you seek when you dream of happiness; he is waiting for you when nothing else you find satisfies you; he is the beauty to which you are so attracted; it is he who provokes you with that thirst for fullness that will not let you settle for compromise; it is he who urges you to shed the masks of a false life; it is he who reads in your hearts your most genuine choices, the choices that others try to stifle. It is Jesus who stirs in you the desire to do something great with your lives, the will to follow an ideal, the refusal to allow yourselves to be ground down by mediocrity, the courage to commit yourselves humbly and patiently to improving yourselves and society, making the world more human and more fraternal.

—Pope Saint John Paul II[*]

I sat on cold stone pavement in the dark, resting against a stone wall. Directly in front of me was an altar surrounded by holy images and ancient icons. Candles continuously burned

---

[*] Address of the Holy Father John Paul II, 15th World Youth Day, Vigil of Prayer (Tor Vergata, August 19, 2000), no. 5, http://w2.vatican.va/content/john-paul-ii/en/speeches/2000/jul-sep/documents/hf_jp-ii_spe_20000819_gmg-veglia.html.

as I stared at a spot on the floor beneath the altar. In the silence, the words of Jesus ran through my head: "Father, into your hands I commit my spirit!" (Lk 23:46). I was looking directly at the spot of Jesus' great sacrifice—the same spot where his Cross was driven into the ground, the Cross from which he hung until he breathed his last. I was in the Church of the Holy Sepulchre, built in Jerusalem over both Calvary and the tomb of Jesus Christ.

The night before his Crucifixion, in the Garden of Gethsemane, Jesus had prayed to his Father: "Father, if you are willing, remove this chalice from me; nevertheless not my will, but yours, be done" (Lk 22:42). Not *my* will—but *your* will be done.

In the last chapter, we looked at the Parable of the Prodigal Son. When the son came back home, his father welcomed him, not as a slave, but as a beloved son. This is true about us: When we come to the Father, he welcomes us as his dearly beloved children. Regardless of our history, regardless of our current struggles, regardless of whatever ways in which we may fail in the future, the Father welcomes us back home not as slaves or guests but as members of the family.

What the parable doesn't mention is what happens *after* the prodigal son is welcomed back. The expectation and the implication is that, once home, the son, like us, should *live* as a son or a daughter of the Father. There is a certain element of surrender involved here. One of our major tasks in the spiritual life is being willing to accept the Father's love for us. But that's just the beginning.

Once we learn how to accept the Father's love, then we hear the call of the Son of God: "Come, follow me" (Lk 18:22). You are called to be a disciple. You are called to live as a son or a daughter of God. But first you must receive the Father's love for you.

When I was about fifteen years old I received one of those little green *New Testaments and Psalms* that the Gideons give away. I was excited to have a Bible of my own and started reading it immediately. At one point, I reached chapter 16 of the Gospel of Matthew where the subheading reads "The Conditions of Discipleship." Here, Jesus gets serious about the expectations of belonging to him: "If any man would come after me, let him deny himself and take up his cross and follow me" (v. 24).

Those words struck me. I might have only been fifteen years old, but those words just *rocked* me. I thought, "This is what it is to be a disciple: to deny myself, to pick up my cross, and to follow after Jesus." Again, let's be clear, the first step is to accept the truth that I am loved. But the next step is denying myself when my will conflicts with the Father's will.

This doesn't mean that a Christian has to say no to every single pleasure or desire. After all, God is the one who invented every pleasure that exists, and he wants to fulfill the true desires of our hearts triumphantly. As C.S. Lewis once put it: "It would seem that Our Lord finds our desires not too strong, but too weak. We are half-hearted creatures, fooling about with drink and sex and ambition when infinite joy is offered us, like an ignorant child who wants to go on making mud pies in a slum because he cannot imagine what is meant by the offer of a holiday at the sea. We are far too easily pleased."[1] But we must say no to our desires when they conflict with the Father's will. At first glance, being a disciple

---

[1] C.S. Lewis, "The Weight of Glory," in *The Weight of Glory and Other Addresses*, rev. ed. (New York: HarperOne; HarperCollins, 2001), 26.

may seem like a recipe for pain, that if we want to follow Jesus then we must get used to a life of saying no. But is this the case? Isn't there something deeper? Isn't there something more?

There is another place where Jesus describes what it's like to be a disciple. Jesus says, "Come to me, all who labor and are heavy laden, and I will give you rest. Take my yoke upon you, and learn from me; for I am gentle and lowly in heart, and you will find rest for your souls. For my yoke is easy, and my burden is light" (Mt 11:28–30).

"Take my yoke upon you, and learn from me." What does this mean? As you may know, a yoke is a piece of farming equipment made out of either wood or metal that goes around the neck or shoulders of a beast of burden. Typically, there are two places in the yoke designated for two animals. The two animals place their heads and necks through the yoke in order to pull a load side by side. Jesus shares his yoke with us; he invites us to work side by side with him.

But what does taking up the yoke mean? A Scripture scholar once pointed out to me that to take another's yoke upon one's self meant to share a worldview with the other. In this particular case, it would mean to share the same worldview as Jesus. If someone took the yoke of Jesus upon himself, he would stand side by side with Jesus, looking at the world in the same way.

How does Jesus look at the world? First, Jesus looks at the world as something fallen and in need of redemption but worth saving. Next, he sees that human beings possess great worth and that they're worth dying for.

On top of this worldview, we are also called to see the Father as Jesus does. So much of our lives can be spent in distrust of the Father. I don't know how many times I have spoken with someone who tells me that he simply does not trust God. Sometimes this is someone who was raised in the Church, someone raised on the Scriptures, someone who knows all the prayers, and someone who went to Mass every Sunday.

On the other hand, Jesus *profoundly* trusted his Father, even when he faced imminent torture and death. For in the Garden of Gethsemane, he prayed, "My Father, if it be possible, let this chalice pass from me; nevertheless, not as I will, but as thou wilt" (Mt 26:39). One of the most important messages that Jesus communicated to us is that we can trust our Father in Heaven. Yet still one of our biggest difficulties is trusting God.

Recall the beginning of the story of the Fall in the Book of Genesis (3:1–24). Adam and Eve are in the Garden. God has shown himself to be their Father. He has created them, cared for them, fed them, and invited them to live with him. But the serpent comes into the Garden and begins to challenge Eve's trust in the Father. The serpent doesn't test Eve's *belief* in God's existence, but her *obedience* to him. Does she trust that God only wants the best for her when he prohibits her from eating the fruit of the tree of knowledge of good and evil lest she dies? Satan says, "You will not die. For God knows that when you eat of it your eyes will be opened, and you will be like God, knowing good and evil" (vv. 4–5), implying, "God doesn't *want* you to be like him; God doesn't want your good. He's not your Father." So Eve (and then Adam) give in to this temptation to doubt the fatherhood of God. In reaching out for the fruit, she refuses to obey the God who has only shown her love and generosity. Ever since this Fall, we've all struggled to trust in God in loving obedience.

A story that demonstrates how we can trust the Father is the story of Abraham, whom God directed to offer his son

Isaac as a sacrifice (Gen 22:1–18). Many people, when they read this story, think, "That is absolutely nuts! Why would God ever ask a father to sacrifice one of his children?" In fact, this is the idea that's conveyed in the recent TV miniseries *The Bible*. In that series, when God instructs Abraham to sacrifice Isaac, Abraham obeys with great reluctance and even groans, "No . . . no!" Isaac is portrayed as being a naïve and unwilling victim when his father drags him to the top of the mountain, binds him, and moves to sacrifice him.

Meanwhile, back at the camp, Sarah (Abraham's wife and Isaac's mother) pieces together what is happening and races to the foot of the mountain where the sacrifice is taking place, seemingly to stop her crazed husband from killing her son.

In the miniseries, as Sarah sees Abraham walking down the mountain (but can't see Isaac), she is visibly grieved and sobs. But then, since Isaac had been spared (by God) at the site of the sacrifice, Sarah sees him as he steps out from behind his father. Then comes a key moment. Sarah cries out to her boy, who looks up and begins running to her. Abraham reaches out to hold his son, but Isaac brushes away his father's hand (after all, he's crazy and almost just killed him!) and runs away from the father to Sarah.

The message of that scene (as it was filmed and edited for the TV series) was essentially "You cannot trust your Father." But this is the *opposite* of the story the Bible conveys. In fact, the story portrays a son and father who deeply trust each other and work together. At the time of the sacrifice of Isaac, Abraham was over one hundred years old. He was not a strong man, and Isaac was not a small boy. Scripture tells us he was strong enough to carry the wood for the sacrifice. Now this is going to be a burnt offering, what is referred to in Jewish tradition as a *holocaust*. Apparently, Isaac was strong enough to carry enough wood to burn a human body. This means that he would have been a strong young man, while Abraham was a frail old man.

Why is this distinction important? It means that when Abraham binds Isaac and lays him on the altar, he is not overpowering Isaac. Isaac is not naïve or unwilling; instead, he is cooperating with Abraham. This is the story of Isaac, the son, who trusts in Abraham, his father. It prefigures Jesus' sacrifice on Calvary. Both stories are about the son trusting the father. In order to have faith, you must trust the other. To put it another way, to have faith is to surrender in love to the other.

We are all called to surrender in love to the Father. Jesus says to everyone: "Come to me. . . . Take my yoke upon you, and learn from me" (Mt 11:29). We are called to learn that we can trust the Father.

We all struggle with trust at times. People who are raised in the Church often hear about rules before experiencing a real relationship with God. Because of this, they can come to view God more as a tyrant than as a Father. I think that there are too many Catholics who are acquainted with the moral directives given by God, but who have never known the God who gives them. I think that there are too many Catholics who have never encountered a God of love, whose every command and directive leads us to a life of love. As a result, their idea of God is too small. But the whole of the Scripture teaches us to see God as a loving and trustworthy Father—a Father who desires that we live in his home and in his heart.

What does this have to do with us right now? First, realize that we can trust the Father. Second, realize that we are called to follow the Son, to say yes to love. To trust the Father means that we understand that he is the one who knows who we really are, and that all his directions for us will lead us to our true identity. Part of following the Son (and saying yes to love) is walking the road with Jesus, who shows us the path that will lead us to our true selves; and that means saying no to certain things.

Live Like This Is Home

What is it to let God be the Lord of your life? As we saw earlier, when the lost son came home, he had a decision: He could live at home as a slave, or he could live there as a son. If he decided to live in his father's home, however, he had to live as part of the family. The same goes for us: We can live in the Church while rejecting the Church's teaching, or we can live in the Church and embrace the Church's teaching. Choosing the latter leads us to ourselves, and to the Church—and the Father—embracing us.

Christians say things like "Jesus is Lord!" But what does it mean? Obviously, a key part of this statement refers to the particular identity of Jesus of Nazareth: he is the Lord of Heaven and Earth. That's the objective fact. On a practical and personal level, it means that we acknowledge him as the actual captain of our lives; we go where he leads us. He gets to be the actual shepherd of our lives; we come when he calls us by name. If we follow Jesus as the true Lord of our lives, then we have to respond accordingly when he asks us to act—or not act.

Before the Parable of the Lost (Prodigal) Son (see Lk 15:11–32), there is the Parable of the Lost Sheep (cf. Lk 15:1–7). This is the story of the good shepherd who leaves the ninety-nine sheep in order to find and recover the one sheep that wandered off—or ran away. Jesus says, "When [the shepherd] has found [the sheep], he lays it on his shoulders, rejoicing" (Lk 15:5). If you've been lost and you've let Jesus find you, then you should know that he desires to place you on his shoulders, and carry you home with joy. So why not let him find you?

Exceptionalism

In 2011, a friend of mine named Andrew had to go to a treatment facility for his alcoholism. The facility had an exercise room, and a sign clearly stated that cardio equipment could only be used for twenty minutes at a time. Now, Andrew is very intense and is very fit, so he knew that twenty minutes wouldn't cut it. He thought to himself, "Twenty minutes might be fine for *most* people, but most people don't compete in Ironman Triathlons. I am the exception to the rule." One day, a fellow patient came up to him and said, "Hey, man, did you see the sign that says you can only use the equipment for twenty minutes at a time?" Andrew bristled and began to say, "Yeah, but—" The other man interrupted him, saying, "So why are you the exception to the rule?"

At that moment, Andrew realized that it wasn't just about using the treadmill. He realized that he had defined his life by being "the exception to the rule." He had always seen *his* issues as different from everyone else's. Because of this, the rules never seemed to apply to him. He always had a reason why he was the exception.

I have found that a person's experience of sexual orientation can be a potent source of *exceptionalism*. I often hear, "Well yes, I know I need to follow Jesus. I know he needs to be the Lord of my life. *But*, I experience these attractions, and therefore I am exempt from Christ's commandment to being chaste. Because I experience this, I am the exception to the rule."

We all have this tendency to seek an exemption. We all have the temptation to excuse ourselves or overlook the rules *in our case*, often self-editing our own stories. "That doesn't apply to me; my story is different." True, we *are* each unique, but what we're all called to is universal. We're all called to love in freedom and truth, and to witness real and powerful love. There is no one whom Jesus doesn't call. What is the call? To love the Lord with all your heart and soul, and to be loved by him.

Some Christians have fallen into the trap of thinking that this simply means repression. Christianity is *only* "deny yourself." Discipleship is merely saying no. Yet this needs to be made eminently clear: To follow Christ is to say *yes* to something. A disciple says yes to *Someone* who gives life and love. Love is not worth anything if there is no denial involved. Consider anyone who is committed to another person. In order for him (or her) to say yes with his whole life, whether that yes is to a spouse, to a parent, to a child, or to a friend, it means he has to be able to say no to himself at times. People who marry are saying no to millions of potential mates. But the reason is the opposite of negative: it is because there is a massive yes that is filling their thoughts.

I sometimes marvel at my brothers-in-law. I am amazed by their ability to deny themselves out of love for their children and their wives. I can see that they are often exhausted and would very much like to rest. But in order to say yes to their wives and to their children, they say no to themselves. This is not repression; they understand that when they say no to themselves, they are saying yes to something greater.

Many people in our culture believe we only have two options when it comes to our sexual desires: we can either repress these desires, ignoring them completely and pretending

they don't exist until they explode, or we can indulge such
desires. Neither of these is a recipe for holiness. Neither is a
recipe for happiness. The Christian way is the choice to say
yes to a greater love. Pope Benedict called this the "path of
renunciation."[2] You might also call this the path of *surrender*.

In the 1600s, there was a young man by the name of Iñigo.
He grew up in northern Spain, a short distance from the coast.
As a native Basque, a people known for their bravery and
fighting prowess, he desired with his whole heart to be one
of the great Spanish heroes. He desired glory; he desired to
be noble and courageous in battle so that people might know
his name throughout his country. Moved by this desire, Iñigo
was fierce and courageous in battle. At one point, however, he
was struck in the thigh by a cannon ball, which shattered his
femur. While he was recovering, all he could think about was
getting back to health, getting back into battle, and getting
back to making a name for himself. But God had other plans
for this fiery and passionate man.

Iñigo loved to read stories of knights, valor, and bravery.
Unfortunately, he must have thought, the home in which he
was convalescing only had two books available. One was on
the lives of the saints and the other was on the life of Christ.
As he began to read these books, his heart was set aflame. He
had grown up in a Christian world, and he knew of the saints,
but as he lay there healing, he realized that he was fighting for
a prize too small. He had been struggling to make a name for
himself, while Jesus Christ was calling him to surrender his
life to the Father's will. God was calling Iñigo to surrender

---

[2]   Benedict XVI, encyclical letter *Deus Caritas Est* (December 25, 2005), no. 5,
http://w2.vatican.va/content/benedict-xvi/en/encyclicals/documents/hf_ben-xvi_
enc_20051225_deus-caritas-est.html.

and place his life under the shepherding, the lordship, the generalship of Christ. He was being called to surrender.

This surrender is not the same thing as suspending or rejecting one's mind or strength. Instead, Christian surrender is to place all of one's intellect, all of one's strength, all of one's heart, and all of one's desires at the service of another. To surrender is to place all of one's self, including one's powers, at God's disposal.

Iñigo started out with a desire for his own personal glory, but ended up surrendering his life to God. In doing so, Jesus reformed and transformed his desire. Iñigo's desire for personal glory became a desire for God's glory. In fact, when Saint Ignatius of Loyola, as he came to be known, founded the Society of Jesus (the Jesuit order), their motto became *Ad Majorem Dei Gloriam* (For the Greater Glory of God). For Ignatius, surrender did not mean that he ceased to be himself. Surrender was not mere repression of his desires. Instead, surrender meant that his desires were *transformed* under the lordship of Jesus Christ. Through this surrender, his desires were amplified and perfected.

The same thing can happen with our sexual desires. We all have different sexual desires. Some are healthy, others not so much. But if we surrender our sexual desires to the lordship of Jesus, they, too, can be perfected and transformed.

In talking with some of my friends who identify as gay and lesbian, I've heard, "Well, there's no one like me in the Church." And I would say that they might be right. It is very possible that there is no one like them in the Church, and maybe this is an indication that the Church *needs them*. Jesus desires that we take up his yoke and follow him, not because the Church needs people who will change doctrine from the inside, but because the Church needs saints. The

Church needs people who are willing to let their minds be transformed, people just like my aforementioned friends who will allow their lives to be transformed and, in this way, to be able to help others. Jesus is not calling anyone to a life of repression or to a life of indulgence; instead, all are called to the narrow path to our true identities, a path where he walks shoulder to shoulder with us.

CHAPTER NINE

Same-Sex Attractions in the Church

"Would you consider marrying me?" Alan, the young man who had just proposed, looked into the eyes of one of his best friends, a young woman named Joan. The year was 1941, and the two were working on a secret government project in Bletchley Park, England. Surprised, Joan looked into Alan's eyes as he gazed at her steadily beneath his trimmed brown hair; and she immediately said yes.

Alan Turing was a genius, a mathematician, and a computer scientist recruited by the British government to design a code-breaking machine. His story was made popular by the movie *The Imitation Game* starring Benedict Cumberbatch as Alan Turing and Keira Knightley as his one-time fiancée Joan Clarke. The day after proposing, while out for a walk after lunch, Alan turned to Joan and said, "I guess you should know . . . I have . . . homosexual tendencies."

Even though Alan Turing and Joan Clarke were part of the team responsible for developing a code-breaking machine known as Christopher, they were unable to be heroes in their own country. In fact, Turing's story only became known when, in 1952, he was arrested by British authorities and tried for indecency because he had homosexual relations with a man named Arnold Murray. The consequence of being found guilty was devastating for Turing. At thirty-nine years old, he underwent chemical castration in the form of estrogen injections, which caused him to experience other side effects. Roughly a year after his hormone treatments ended, on June 7, 1954, Turing killed himself. Alone in his apartment building, he ate half of an apple that he had injected with cyanide. The tragedy of Turing's story is that it is not rare. According to the Federal Bureau of Investigation, in 2013 roughly 20 percent of hate crimes in the United States were based on perceived sexual orientation.[1] This places hate-related violence against homosexuals the second most common hate-related crime (behind those that are motivated by race, above those motivated by religion). In addition, it is claimed that "sexual minority youth are among those most likely to report suicidality (suicidal thoughts, plans, and attempts)."[2]

The Catholic Church is concerned with the safety and care of all people, regardless of what they are experiencing or why, although some might claim that whatever the Church has to say about this issue is a little hypocritical.

In the spring of 2002, I was preparing to be ordained a transitional deacon in the Catholic Church. In the United States, that spring was known as "The Long Lent" after allegations and evidence of priestly sexual misconduct against minors (and the subsequent covering up of such misconduct by some Catholic bishops) hit the newspapers. It seemed that everywhere I turned there were more and more stories of priests who had abused children and of Church authorities who did little or nothing to stop them. In light of

---

[1]　"Hate Crime Statistics," Federal Bureau of Investigation, 2013, https://ucr.fbi.gov/hate-crime/2013/topic-pages/incidents-and-offenses/incidentsandoffenses_final.

[2]　Stephen T. Russell, "Sexual Minority Youth and Suicide Risk," *American Behavioral Scientist* 46, no. 9 (May 2003): 1241.

these cases, it might seem hypocritical for the Church to say anything with regard to her teaching on sex. I realize that the terrible decisions of a small number of priests and bishops who have gone before me might seem to render anything the Church has to say on any moral issue invalid, but I ask for wisdom and maturity here. Those crimes were done *in spite of* and *in violation of* the Church's teaching on human dignity and sexuality.

The fact is, despite the impression you may get from media, not every leader in the Church is a failure or hypocrite, even though none of us is perfect. The Church points us to Christ, who is the answer to every possible problem that the world faces and the fulfillment of every genuinely human desire: we gain everything and lose nothing except fear and death by becoming his disciples. Yes, there are many in the Church who deny or betray Jesus, an old pattern that goes back to Judas. But Jesus predicted this. We should not let it keep us from the radiant truths of the Gospel, truths that are worth everything to possess. Besides, if the Church were only filled with perfect people, we wouldn't be allowed in.

A year before his death in 1321, Dante Alighieri completed his masterpiece, *The Divine Comedy*. In it, different guides lead Dante out of Hell, through Purgatory, and into Paradise. Most people stop at the *Inferno* or the *Purgatorio*, the first two books of *The Divine Comedy*, and fail to read *Paradiso* (which might reveal something about our preoccupation with sin over grace, but that's beside the point). The *Inferno* describes the nine circles of Hell, each circle being associated with a different deadly sin. The deeper and deeper a person goes down into Hell, into the *Inferno*, the worse the sins are. The sin of treachery and betrayal is in the deepest, darkest, coldest circle of Hell, where Lucifer resides. The circle before this is fraud. The seventh circle is violence; the sixth, heresy; the fifth, anger; the fourth, greed; the third, gluttony. The second circle from the top is the circle of lust. In representing Hell as a pit with descending circles of worsening sins, Dante Alighieri accurately portrayed something that is very important: while sins of lust are deadly, there are deadlier sins. The sin of pride, for example, which would prevent a person from allowing God's mercy to forgive and heal his soul, is considered a deadlier sin.

In his book *Mere Christianity*, C. S. Lewis notes:

> Finally, though I have had to speak at some length about sex, I want to make it as clear as I possibly can that the centre of Christian morality is not here. If anyone thinks that Christians regard unchastity as the supreme vice, he is quite wrong. The sins of the flesh are bad, but they are the least bad of all sins. All the worst pleasures are purely spiritual: the pleasure of putting other people in the wrong, of bossing and patronising and spoiling sport, and back-biting; the pleasures of power, of hatred. For there are two things inside me, competing with the human self which I must try to become. They are the Animal self, and the Diabolical self. The Diabolical self is the worse of the two. That is why a cold, self-righteous prig who goes regularly to church may be far nearer to hell than a prostitute. But, of course, it is better to be neither.[3]

Far from being obsessed with sex, the Catholic Church teaches that there are far worse sins that a person can commit. Still, all persons are called to chastity, which means that all of us are called to love well and to love according to the truth. In the *Catechism of the Catholic Church* (*CCC*), the Church expresses this in these words:

---

[3] C. S. Lewis, *Mere Christianity* (New York: HarperCollins, 2009), 132.

Charity is the *form* of all the virtues. Under its influence, chastity appears as a school of the gift of the person. Self-mastery is ordered to the gift of self. Chastity leads him who practices it to become a witness to his neighbor of God's fidelity and loving kindness. The virtue of chastity blossoms in *friendship*. (*CCC* 2346–47; emphasis in original)

"Under its influence, chastity appears as a school of the gift of the person." Love is becoming a gift; it is willing the good of the other. "Self-mastery is ordered to the gift of the self," meaning, if I can't do what I want to do, if I can't do what I know I am made to do, if I am not in charge of myself—I am not free. If I want to love *freely*, I have to learn how. This means that chastity is not an end in itself. Instead, chastity allows us to love better and to become better *witnesses* to God's love for the world.

And yet chastity is the least popular of all the virtues. In the words of C. S. Lewis:

Chastity is the most unpopular of the Christian virtues. There is no getting away from it. The old Christian rule is either marriage with complete faithfulness to your partner or else total abstinence. Now this is so difficult and so contrary to our instincts that obviously either Christianity is wrong or our sexual instinct as it now is has gone wrong. One or the other. Of course, being a Christian, I think it's the *instinct* that has gone wrong.[4]

Here, C. S. Lewis is pointing out that sexual desire is not bad. In fact, as *eros*, it is oriented toward moving us out of ourselves. Unfortunately, sexual desire "gone wrong" doesn't move us out of ourselves to become a gift of self. Instead, it often causes us to recoil back into ourselves and use other people for our own selfish pleasure.

---

[4] Ibid., 127, emphasis added.

Homosexuality is nothing new in the Catholic Church. Since the beginning of the Church, there have been brothers and sisters in Christ who experience homosexual desires. Imagine Saint Paul looking out at his community of believers in the city of Corinth—a first-century version of Las Vegas, New York, and Amsterdam all rolled into one. To "live like a Corinthian" was a common insult, meaning that a person was willing to do virtually anything when it came to lust. Saint Paul revealed to the Corinthians their great dignity and their great call. He had told them the truth of their origin, their story, and their destiny. Many no doubt had checkered pasts, wounded pasts, and many were currently wounded, carrying various burdens. He knew these men and women well, and he knew their struggles and experiences. This is why he wrote to his beloved brothers and sisters in Corinth these words:

> Do you not know that the unrighteous will not inherit the kingdom of God? Do not be deceived; neither the immoral, nor idolaters, nor adulterers, nor homosexuals, nor thieves, nor the greedy, nor drunkards, nor revilers, nor robbers will inherit the kingdom of God. And such were some of you. But you were washed, you were sanctified, you were justified in the name of the Lord Jesus Christ and in the Spirit of our God. (1 Cor 6:9–11)

Now let's pay attention to this. Saint Paul goes through this list of sins that some people in the Corinthian church had committed. Which sins? Only sexual sins? Well, he knew these folks (and he knew Corinth), so those sexual sins are certainly on the list. About half of the sins on the list are associated with sex. The other half, however, are sins not associated with sex, such as stealing, greed, excessive drinking, and gossiping. Clearly, Saint Paul is not obsessed with sex.

Saint Paul is reminding the Corinthians who have committed these sins that they are not defined by their pasts or by their sins because they have been washed clean in the Sacrament of Baptism. He reminds them that they should not allow these past things to define them because they are made *new* through their relationship with Christ.

Church teaching on sexuality is often misunderstood. In the *Catechism of the Catholic Church*, which is a summary of the Church's official teaching, there are only *three brief paragraphs* on the issue of homosexuality. All of them are connected to the Church's profound teaching that every human being has dignity. So what does the Church *actually* teach?

First, she *defines* homosexuality:

> Homosexuality refers to relations between men or between women who experience an exclusive or predominant sexual attraction toward persons of the same sex. (*CCC* 2357)

Then, in the following sentence, she tells us:

> It [homosexuality] has taken a great variety of forms through the centuries and in different cultures.

The Church, in the passage above, clearly acknowledges that homosexuality isn't something new. In fact, homosexuality is mentioned in the first book of the Bible—Genesis—in the story of Sodom and Gomorrah (Gen 19:1–29).

The *Catechism* then goes on to state:

> Its psychological genesis remains largely unexplained. (*CCC* 2357)

When it comes to the issue of whether same-sex attractions are a result of nature, or nurture, or some combination of the two, the Church wisely refrains from determining the issue. This is partly because current research on the topic is inconclusive. But more importantly, it is because the chief concern of the Church, in the

area of sexuality as well is in all other areas, is to present Christ's
way of love in action for all her members. It is again a question
of how our identity is determined. The Church understands
our identity to be sons and daughters of God, whatever our
circumstances or experiences may have been. That identity is
liberating for all of us and calls us to loving deeds.

Next, the Church states:

> Basing itself on Sacred Scripture, which presents homosexual *acts* as
> acts of grave depravity (cf. Gn 19:1–29; Rom 1:24–27; 1 Cor 6:10; 1
> Tim 1:10), tradition has always declared that "homosexual *acts* are
> intrinsically disordered" (CDF [Congregation for the Doctrine of the
> Faith], *Persona humana* 8).They are contrary to the natural law. They
> close the sexual act to the gift of life. (*CCC* 2357; emphasis added)

Now, the terms "disordered" and "grave depravity" might
sound harsh. But it is important to remember that these terms
are used to describe the *act* itself; they aren't a description of
the *person.*

Love, when it's ordered rightly, wants the good of the
other. But when it's ordered wrongly, love pursues one's own
selfish desire. To put it another way, we are all made for truth
as well as for love, yet all of us have experienced the disordered
desire to lie. We are all called to honor others, but when we are
tempted to gossip about another, this is a disordered desire.

Moving on:

> They [homosexual acts] do not proceed from a genuine affective
> and sexual complementarity. (*CCC* 2357)

The Church points back to the natural law. Paying attention to
the nature of things (even basic biology), the Church affirms
that homosexual actions between men or between women do
not reflect the complementarity implied by human sexuality,

including the biological and even affective bonding of male and female; instead, such actions thwart the fulfillment of the sexual act's intrinsic ends—*what-it-is-for-ness*.

The *Catechism* goes on to explain,

> Under no circumstances can they [the actions] be approved. (*CCC* 2357)

And,

> The number of men and women who have deep-seated homosexual tendencies is not negligible. (*CCC* 2358)

Here, the Church insists that no matter how *many* people there are who experience same-sex attractions, we must not overlook them. Our churches, our cities, and our families include any number of men and women who are same-sex attracted and we need to be aware of it.

It sometimes happens that people change their position regarding the Church's teaching concerning homosexual acts because a friend or family member identifies as gay or lesbian. This fascinates me. When someone tells me his views have changed because of this, I want to ask, "How? In what way? *Why*?" If this person responds that he has become nicer to that individual who came out, I'm curious to know how he treated that individual previously. Did he dislike that person before? I am happy when negative views have changed, but it becomes problematic if the person who changed starts believing that homosexual acts are no longer wrong.

There are several problems with this change. First, it is a little shallow. Just because someone you love wants to do something wrong, you are willing to say that it's okay? Have you really thought this through?

Second, it is *really* shallow. Honestly. If my relative or friend desires to act in a certain way, should I be willing to abandon my faith in order to show that person my support? Am I truly a believer if I am willing to void the tenets of my faith because someone I know or love ignores those tenets?

The *Catechism* goes on to make an important point:

> This inclination, which is objectively disordered, constitutes for most of them a trial. (*CCC* 2358)

I remember speaking with a young man who had recently identified himself as gay. In the course of our conversation, he made it very clear that if he had a choice, he wouldn't have same-sex attractions, saying, "Do you think that I chose to be gay?" I responded, "Of course not. Do you think that I think that?" He looked at me right in the eyes and he said, "I would never choose this for myself."

Many of the homosexual men and women I meet feel the same way as the young man above: being same-sex attracted is felt to be a burden and a trial. At the same time, there are those who outwardly advertise their homosexuality as the best thing to happen to them. They see it as part of their identity that they thank God for. Yet even these men and women, many of whom I've known, admit that their homosexuality has been a trial at many stages of their lives.

> They must be accepted with respect, compassion, and sensitivity. Every sign of unjust discrimination in their regard should be avoided. (*CCC* 2358)

Some people may believe that the Church's teachings on homosexuality result in violence and discrimination against our brothers and sisters. Yet, what *is* the official teaching of the Church? It's *not* that people must be merely *tolerated*; instead, the Church teaches that homosexual people *must be accepted* with respect, compassion, and sensitivity. The

Church *commands* acceptance of men and women who have same-sex attractions. The Church wants to make a clear and definite point that she is on the side of every individual.

Homosexual persons "are called to fulfill God's will in their lives, and, if they are Christian, to unite to the sacrifice of the Lord's Cross the difficulties they may encounter from their condition" (*CCC* 2358).

What does it mean to unite one's difficulties to the sacrifice of the Lord's Cross?

When people are in the midst of pain, there are often no arguments or explanations that will help them to make sense of their suffering. There is often just the hurt.

Nothing I write here is meant to be dismissive; there is no simple answer to the problem of human suffering. In fact, the *Catechism* states that there is no element of the Christian story that is not, in part, a response to the problem of evil (*CCC* 309), the problem that includes the issue of human pain.

But there are some principles taught by Christ that can help us approach pain. Regardless of our circumstances, we all need to learn these principles because all of us will experience pain and suffering. If we don't know why or where God fits into this, not only could we fall into the trap of allowing our pain to drive a wedge between ourselves and God, but we will miss out on the power in the suffering.

First, we need to understand that God does not directly will suffering. He did not make evil and cannot will evil. In fact, evil is not even considered a "thing" or a kind of being.

This is not a random side point. God only wills the good. Then what is evil? Evil is either the absence of a good or a distortion of a good. For example, the physical evil of blindness is not a thing in itself; it is the *lack* of a good thing (sight). Likewise, gluttony is the *distortion* or a disorder of a good thing (eating).

The moment that God created a world outside of himself, and created beings who have free will, he allowed for the possibility that those free beings could choose evil. God never directly wills evil, but he allows evil because he prizes freedom and what freely choosing beings can become if they choose to act toward the proper goal or end—what genuinely fulfills their human nature.

Unfortunately, sometimes free beings choose to misuse freedom. And others are misled or harmed by others' abuses and misdeeds. At other times we simply don't know the "why" behind the evil we encounter or the suffering we experience.

I understand if this response doesn't make everything better. We *still* suffer, and evil *still* happens. Someone might ask, "What does it matter if God has directly willed it or merely allowed it?"

Well, for one thing, it reminds us that God is absolutely Good. He is not, as Eve was tempted to believe, a tyrant. He is a perfect, all-loving Father. Further, it reminds us that God has the ability to bring good out of evil. Consider the Old Testament story of Joseph in chapter 37 of Genesis. God was able to use the evil of Joseph's brothers selling him into slavery to bring about the good of saving the people of Israel and of reconciling Joseph and his brothers. Another example is when God allowed Saint Paul to be thrown into jail, but Paul said it offered him the chance to proclaim Jesus (see Phil 1:13). But of course the greatest example is of the Father allowing his Son to suffer and die in order to bring about the salvation of the world. Jesus didn't want to suffer—which is why he prayed so intensely in the Garden of Gethsemane. But he wanted to do what the Father wanted, even if that meant taking on himself the sins of the world. He accepted his suffering so it could bring about the good of the world's redemption and so he could demonstrate his deep love for the Father and for us (see Lk 22:42–44). In the end, his suffering led to the Resurrection, by which Jesus became the head of a new human family.

The Bible reveals a number of possible reasons God would allow us to suffer, although these reasons are not always obvious in every experience of suffering.

Suffering can be a consequence of bad decisions. In biblical terms, this is called "reaping what you sow" (cf. Gal 6:7–8). We may have brought suffering upon ourselves or others due to bad choices (cf. Rom 6:23). We may also suffer due to the bad decisions of others. (God sometimes acts to prevent harm to us from others. But if he *always* protected us from the bad decisions of others, then human freedom would be seriously compromised.)

Suffering can be a remedy. There are times when God allows us to experience suffering in order to wake us up and draw our attention to him (cf. Heb 12:4–5). C. S. Lewis put it this way: "We can ignore even pleasure. But pain insists upon being attended to. God whispers to us in our pleasures, speaks to us in our conscience, but shouts in our pains: it is his megaphone to rouse a deaf world."[5]

Suffering can be a teacher. Pain can also bring us wisdom. Suffering can be a teacher (cf. Eph 5:26–27; Ps 119:67; Jas 1:2–4). This truth is revealed in the Bible but is made visible in people of great wisdom; they have suffered and have allowed their suffering to bring them to a depth of understanding of

---

[5] C. S. Lewis, *The Problem of Pain* (New York: HarperOne, 2001), 91.

themselves and the human experience that would have been impossible without it.

But beyond acting as a remedy or a teacher, suffering with Christ has a power all its own. Saint Paul writes of this when he says, "Now I rejoice in my sufferings for your sake, and in my flesh I complete what is lacking in Christ's afflictions for the sake of his body, that is, the Church" (Col 1:24).

This means that suffering can be redemptive. There is another meaning to suffering, which we touched on already when we looked at the examples of Jesus and Saint Paul. Suffering was God's chosen means to redeem the world. Because evil had to be dealt with and in justice could not be waved away, and because humanity had incurred serious self-inflicted wounds that were killing us but that we could not heal on our own, God willingly took upon himself our condition. The suffering of Jesus—the God-Man—his walking through darkness and even death to the triumph of rising from the dead, has made salvation available to every person. In accomplishing our salvation, God didn't simply take away our suffering, not yet; instead, he transformed it. God's willingness to embrace suffering out of love has given suffering a meaning and a power that it did not have. Even more, Jesus has called every person who belongs to him to share in this power. He has invited all who love him to share in his mission.

Pope Saint John Paul II spoke of this transformation and participation of suffering in his encyclical *Salvifici Doloris*:

> Christ has in a sense opened his own redemptive suffering to all human suffering.... Christ has accomplished the world's Redemption through his own suffering. For, at the same time, this Redemption, even though it was completely achieved by Christ's suffering, lives on and in its own special way develops in the history of man. It lives and

develops as the body of Christ, the Church, and in this dimension every human suffering, by reason of the loving union with Christ, completes the suffering of Christ. It completes that suffering *just as the Church completes the redemptive work of Christ.*[6]

What this means is that God is very close to those who suffer with him. Even further, the New Testament and the story of the Church teach that suffering does not reveal a lack of God's love. How does this Christian understanding of redemptive suffering correspond to the topic at hand? "Homosexual persons are called to chastity" (*CCC* 2359).

If we were to delete the first word, this statement would still be true. The Church teaches that *all* persons are called to chastity, not merely homosexual persons. Once again, this is not an *us and them* issue. We're all in the same boat. The virtue of chastity brings to all followers of Christ the freedom to love genuinely; it also entails a measure of suffering in gaining that freedom. All of us experience some kind of disorder in our sexual appetites or in our sexual attractions, and *all* of us are called to turn from those distortions to the loving self-mastery of chastity. "By the virtues of self-mastery that teach them inner freedom, at times by the support of disinterested friendship, by prayer and sacramental grace, they can and should gradually and resolutely approach Christian perfection" (*CCC* 2359).

The primary thing that the Church is saying here is the same message she brings to all her children: that all of us, homosexual men and women included, are called to be saints. Nothing less. In the Catholic Church, the greatest

---

[6] John Paul II, Apostolic Letter on the Christian Meaning of Human Suffering *Salvifici Doloris* (February 11, 1984), no. 24 (emphasis in original), http://w2.vatican.va/content/john-paul-ii/en/apost_letters/1984/documents/hf_jp-ii_apl_11021984_salvifici-doloris.html.

recognition of one's personal sanctity is to be canonized as a saint. Perhaps someday the Catholic Church will canonize a man or woman known to have been a same-sex attracted person, as the Church has canonized others who have overcome challenges to live faithful to God. I and many other Catholics look forward to that day. God's grace is available to each of us who are willing to walk the road of freedom and love with Christ. That road will certainly involve suffering: all Christians are shaped by the Cross, the doorway to Christ's life and healing. All Christians have to "die to self" in order to live for God. What is needed is to be willing to open ways to allow his grace into our lives.

Returning to Saint Paul and his brothers and sisters of the congregation in Corinth, Paul wrote: "And such were some of you. But you were washed, you were sanctified, you were justified in the name of the Lord Jesus Christ and in the Spirit of our God" (1 Cor 6:11). God gives all people hope. The Church offers nothing less than sanctity for *all*. No one is excluded and no one is disqualified, so long as we surrender ourselves to God.

CHAPTER TEN

Dealing with Definitions

A number of years ago, before the Supreme Court ruling on same-sex marriage, Minnesota, the state where I live, debated the issue of marriage. Every time I drove anywhere in Duluth or Saint Paul, I observed lawns with orange and blue signs driven into the grass with slogans like "Vote NO against limiting the freedom to marry!" and "Every person has a right to marry." Every so often, I would see blue and green signs that stated "Vote YES to keep the traditional definition of marriage."

Virtually every evening, there was another news story on the issue of marriage. Everyone seemed to be talking about marriage, or limiting the freedom to marry, or the notion that a person ought to be able to marry whomever he or she chooses. But there was a mysterious absence in all of the discussions: a clear definition of marriage.

At the risk of sounding simplistic, it doesn't make any sense to claim that every person has a right to marry when we are not able to define marriage. Wouldn't you think it important that the state provide a useful definition of marriage when having a vote to redefine it? If we can't clearly say what a thing is, shouldn't the first step be to define that thing? So I want to pose this question: What is marriage?

Marriage Is Unique

What makes marriage a unique relationship in all of mankind, in all of civilization? A little biology will help us answer this question. When observing the human anatomy, we find a number of biological systems. There is the limbic system, the cardiovascular system, the digestive system, the respiratory system, the muscular system, and a few others. Each of these systems is complete and whole.

So in each person's body there is an entire digestive system that functions independently of other humans; and the same is true of the limbic and cardiovascular systems. But there is one biological system every human being has that is *incomplete* on its own: the reproductive system.

The reproductive system is the only biological system that needs another human body in order to function. And that isn't all: It doesn't just need any other human body; it needs a *complementary* body. The male and female bodies are complementary in just the right way. They are alike enough to be the same species, and yet dissimilar enough to be different sexes. Male and female are not incidentally dissimilar, but are significantly dissimilar. They are different in a very precise way. The differences between male and female are oriented toward a very unique *unity* that allows for the possibility of a special kind of wholeness. In order to have this wholeness, a specific human act is needed—biological unity oriented toward the creation of children.

Obviously, there may be a lot of other things people can do with those parts of their bodies, but we'll leave that aside for the moment. A nonbiased, outside observer would recognize that the purpose of the human sexual act is to form a biological unity of a man and a woman, oriented toward the creation of human life.

At this point, someone might say, "Oh, that's nice. So what you're saying is that marriage all comes down to sex." Well, kind of!—and kind of not. Marriage is much more than sex. We recognize that marriage is a union of hearts and minds as well—a permanent and exclusive one, one in which men and women each bring the experiences of their respective sexes to their complementary union. Marriage is also a union of wills. Marriage involves love and commitment. But, and this is important, marriage is not the only human relationship that involves love and commitment. During the course of public discussion on the issue of marriage, I've often heard: "Come on, what's wrong with you? Can't you see that love is love?" Of course it is. But that isn't really saying anything. There are a lot of human relationships that involve love that we don't call marriage. Relationships between siblings and friends can involve real love and concern. But they're not for that reason marriages.

What about *commitment*? There can also be commitment in any number of different human relationships. For example, deep friendships typically involve a deep commitment by both parties. Love between a mother and her daughter can also involve a deep commitment. Even business partnerships can involve a deep commitment.

I participated in a discussion on this topic at a Catholic college that also housed around a hundred religious sisters. These women are deeply committed to God and to each other. This commitment gives them strength and allows them to grow into the women they are meant to be. In their relationships, there is love, commitment, and even mutual assistance and help. But, does that make their particular situation a marriage? Of course not. Even though it has those other elements, it lacks the essential elements that constitute *marriage*.

What if you had two tennis players who were deeply committed to only competing, exclusively, as doubles partners together for the rest of their lives? That's an exclusive relationship of deep commitment. But is it a marriage? No. Still more, what if two people vowed that they would only hold hands with each other for the rest of their lives? Would *that* be a marriage? No. What about something even more unique: What if two people vowed they would only hug each other until the day they died? Again, no, this would not constitute a marriage. At a fundamental level there is an essential, unique action that exists in Matrimony. What is this action? It's the specific human act that results in the biological *unity* that by its nature—its what-it-is-ness—oriented toward the creation of human life. This is the distinguishing characteristic of every marriage.

Changing Games, Changing Names

Consider the game of baseball. There are a lot of things that go into baseball. There are two teams of players, the field, and someone who officiates the game, and there are things like baseball caps, baseball gloves, and uniforms. Now, many of those things can change, right? Any kid who has ever participated in a pick-up game knows this. Rather than the official nine people on a side, you might have only three kids on a team. Rather than the regulation base, you might have bases that are made up of an extra glove, an old car mat, and someone's T-shirt. You can have the regulation-size baseball field, or just space out the bases according to the amount of room you have in your backyard.

Clearly, some elements of baseball can change because they are nonessential. But because there are *some* nonessential things, does that mean that there are *no* essential things? Of course not. In order for baseball to be baseball, at least three things are necessary: First, you need a baseball. Second, you need a bat. And, finally, you need to try to hit the ball with the bat in order to run around the bases and score a run. This is what is needed in order to play the game of baseball.

What happens if you take even one of those essential elements away? You change the game of baseball into something else. If you don't have a bat, you are playing catch. Without a baseball, you may be playing stickball. Maybe you're hitting a softball, but that's a different game too! If you're not circling the bases to score a run, then you might be having batting practice or fielding practice. But what you need to have a baseball game are those three essential elements. Take any one of them away, and you're not playing baseball.

Now along comes a football player and he says, "I want to be a baseball player." You can imagine someone on the baseball team responding, "Awesome! You're on my team, and you're up next." But what if the person says, "No, no, no, I don't like baseball. I don't want to *play* baseball. I just want to be a baseball player. I want to play football, but I want you to call it baseball." Would it be unfair to tell this person that it isn't possible to be a baseball player without playing baseball? No, this is not being unfair, because if you want to be a baseball player you actually have to play baseball. And in order to have the game of baseball, you have to have the three essential elements.

What if the other person objects, "A game is a game. They are the same. I have a team, and you have a team. I play on a field, and you play on a field. You have an official, and I have an official. I even have a uniform, and you have uniforms, and I play with a ball, and you play with a ball. It's the same game!"

Baseball and football are both games, and they are similar in some ways. But they are not the same game.

Morality Police?

When it comes to marriage, there are all sorts of unnecessary, nonessential elements. Without discussing the issue of morality, let's look at what makes marriage *a unique relationship* in all of humanity.

Is it love? No. Lots of relationships have love. Is it commitment? No. Lots of relationships have commitment. What makes marriage unique is that it is a specific union of hearts and wills, culminating in a biological unity that is naturally oriented toward the creation of life. Essentially, marriage is the permanent and exclusive relationship between sexually complementary couples.

Some might argue with this. I recently spoke with a young woman who said, "But what about a couple who can't have children? Are they disqualified? Is that not a marriage?" Yes, because they are engaging in the *act* that is by its nature the kind of act oriented toward the creation of human life, they *are* actually forming a biological unity with every sexual act. Her very thoughtful objection was like the football player pointing toward the baseball team and saying, "That team has never even scored a run. I play football, and I score touchdowns all the time! I am a better baseball player than they are!" And yet, we know that the worst baseball player is more of a baseball player than the best football player.

Hasn't Marriage Evolved Over Time?

Other people might say, "Marriage has changed throughout history. Not only has it changed, but there have been times when certain people, certain races, or certain ethnicities were actually not allowed to marry. This is the same thing; it's just another civil rights issue."

That is an interesting and attractive objection. But it isn't ultimately convincing. For example, those restrictions on who could marry were almost exclusively aimed at retaining a demographic unity or creating demographic diversity. Some cultures prohibited marrying outside of one's own religion, ethnicity, or social group in order to preserve homogeneity. Others prohibited marrying within one's group in order to promote heterogeneity. But the focus was on the type of culture that marriage created, not on the couple themselves.

Just because marriage looks different in different cultures doesn't mean that it's infinitely malleable. Likewise, just because some nonessential elements of baseball can be changed doesn't mean the essential elements have changed.

People also bring up the issue of polygamy. That is understandable, especially since there has been a long history of polygamy in various cultures (even in some religious cultures). Even in situations of polygamy, however, marriage is still between one man and one woman. This is not mere semantics, but how those who practice polygamy perceive and live it. Jack is married to Jill. Jack is *also* married to Jane. But Jill is not married to Jane. This has never been considered to be the case. Even in occasions of polygamy, only a man and a woman are engaging in the biological act that leads toward the unity and to the creation of human life. The essential elements oriented toward what constitutes a marriage are present.

Grammar Police

We've all been the victims of the grammar police. For example, when you asked your English teacher, "Excuse me, can I go to the bathroom?" and the teacher may have responded, "You *can* go, but you *may* not."

The English teacher was trying to point out that there is a difference between "can" and "may." At first glance, the issue of marriage may sound like one of these cases. What it sounds like people are saying to those who want to enter into a same-sex marriage is, "You *may not* do this." Throughout history, that has been the case with racial, religious, or ethnic discrimination. For example, a mixed-race couple, who desired to get married, were told, "You may not enter into marriage." But if they actually got married, would they really be married? Yes! Because they have the essential elements. The state was unfairly saying, "You *may not*," but it didn't have the power to say, "You *cannot*." People of different races and cultures could, in fact, enter into the kind of union we call marriage—a complementary union in which a man and a woman unite together in the kind of act by which new human beings come into the world. They were capable of establishing such a union. It's just that certain societies didn't want men and women from different groups to do so.

But Love Is Love!

Now, again, someone could say that love is love. Well, yes and no. That's like saying a game is a game. Yes, a game is a game. But a baseball game isn't a football game. And marital love isn't the same thing as parental love. And sibling love isn't necessarily the same thing as friendship love. If the definition is going to change, then there needs to be a useful criterion for this change.

Someone might say, "You should be able to marry whomever you love." But where does that lead us? Rather than giving us a new definition for marriage, it merely serves to undefine marriage.

I was speaking with one of my students a while back, and she initially claimed to be fine with undefining marriage. She said, "Well, marriage can mean what you want it to mean *for you*, and it can mean what I want it to mean *for me*." She was claiming that it would be most helpful and most just if we didn't have a shared definition for marriage. Just let people define it for themselves.

This kind of relativism might help people avoid conflict for a short period of time, but communities and cultures don't exist merely to avoid conflict; they exist to bring people into relationship with each other or to help them sustain relationships. Undefining basic terms and concepts helps no one in the long run.

Furthermore, if love is the only criterion for marriage, then I should be able to marry whomever I love. Mark should be able to marry Matt, right? What if Mark and Matt are brothers? Should they *still* be free to marry? Now, I am not equating same-sex actions with incest. I'm simply applying the same criterion that is being used to redefine marriage (love) to another kind of relationship. If love is all you need to redefine marriage, then there is literally no limit to who can get married.

Building Blocks

"But still, why do you care about other people's relationships? What is the big deal? Why does the Church keep getting involved in this? Why are the bishops making such a big deal about this?" We need to slow down long enough to think about this.

We might also ask: "Why is the state so interested in this particular relationship? After all, no one thinks we should get government licenses for our friendships; there is no field of legal thought called 'friendship law' though there is an extensive one called 'marriage law.'" The reason for such high interest in marriage by the state has to do with the recognized social importance of marriage. Most people acknowledge that marriage is the most fundamental building block of any society. The marriage relationship is prior to any other human relationship and as a socially recognized relationship it specially honors the relationship of a man and a woman committed to each other and to any children they may have. Marriage exists before tribes, neighborhoods, or countries. When two people come together in the particular kind of way that involves them giving themselves to each other in a complementary, comprehensive union of life, and which involves the kind of act that brings forth more humans into this world, this is the beginning of tribes, neighborhoods, and countries.

Therefore, marriage is the most fundamental building block of our society. Are we at a place where we are not willing to even pause and consider the implications of changing the essential composition of this social building block? If someone was constructing a building—one that would need to support a great deal of weight and last for a long time—would it be wise to tweak the composition of the foundational blocks and immediately begin construction without testing their resilience? That does not seem to be good engineering.

Likewise, we don't know what might happen to a culture that dramatically changes the composition of its most basic building block.

Marriage has a privileged place in our society, not because we want to help people nurture their romantic relationships as such, but because stable marriages build healthy societies—again, not merely stable romantic relationships, but stable marriages, that is, the kind of permanent and exclusive relationships that honor the kind of union by which new human beings are brought into the world.

Rights?

This chapter is not about rights, but rather about clarifying the meaning of a universally accepted relationship. That said, we can all sympathize with the person who is not allowed into the emergency room with the most important person in his life simply because he doesn't qualify as "immediate family." We can understand the motivation behind unmarried people who share their lives together wanting to receive the tax benefits that married couples receive because they share their lives together.

It might be unjust to deny a person's "life partner" access to a hospital room. Maybe the government should allow people living in relationships besides marriage to receive similar tax benefits as married couples. The Church has no special issue if those laws are changed in reasonable ways. There are approaches to addressing the underlying concerns without declaring as "marriage" relationships different in important ways from the reality of marriage and what marriage honors socially—the union of a man and a woman by which new human beings come to be and society is preserved.

Last Note

Ryan T. Anderson, senior research fellow at the Heritage Foundation, has written extensively on the legal and cultural arguments for the recovery of the traditional definition of marriage. Dan Savage, an author and activist for the LGBT community, has also written and commented on the arguments for the redefinition of marriage in our society. In many ways, their work represents the best arguments for each side.

Remarkably, their strongest arguments are rooted in the same belief. They both posit that over the past fifty years, there has been a de facto redefinition of the traditional institution of marriage as it has been entered into and lived. This is the reason that I examined marriage as an institution that predates today's culture and discussed why its essentials have everything to do with the sexual union oriented toward procreation and education of children: many people today don't live marriage this way.

Dan Savage has argued that, with the legal declaration and cultural acceptance of no-fault divorce and with the separation of marriage from child-rearing, same-sex marriage is merely the natural extension of what already exists. This argument makes sense only if we concede that marriage isn't permanent and isn't by its nature ordered toward new life.

Ryan T. Anderson counters by pointing out that our culture is in a position of heightened awareness of what we have done to marriage. With the case for same-sex marriage being represented to our cultural consciousness, more people are aware of the devastation that our de facto redefinition of marriage has caused. One of his many intelligent arguments is that it is worthwhile to pause and reexamine whether we, as a people, want to continue down this road of redefinition.

CHAPTER ELEVEN

Where Is That in the Bible?

"Did you know that the Bible doesn't actually say anything about homosexuality?" So said a young man who had revealed his same-sex attractions to me, a number of days before. Now, this man had been raised Catholic and really loved his faith. Even though he had experienced same-sex attractions ever since he could remember, it was his faith in Christ, in the Church, and in the Bible that directed his approach to sexuality. But he had recently read a number of articles online and watched a number of YouTube videos. He had even read Matthew Vines' book *God and the Gay Christian*, and he found that there were some people, claiming to be Christian and to be following everything in the Bible, who taught that the Bible was silent on this issue.

Contrary to what some people claim, the Bible is incredibly clear on this question. Sometimes people object to referring to the Old Testament on the subject because, they argue, plenty of things were forbidden in the Old Testament that are permitted in the New Testament. That statement grossly oversimplifies things because there are also things required or forbidden in the Old Testament that are still required or forbidden in the New Testament. The issue isn't whether the Old Testament contains things that Christians should follow—it does. It's a question of how we should understand those things in light of the fuller truth of the New Testament. But since that is a somewhat involved discussion, let's focus on the New Testament's teaching. It is clear in the New Testament that homosexual acts are not permissible.

Writing to the Christians in Rome around A.D. 57, Saint Paul makes a connection between homosexual acts and idolatry. Not that Paul says these two things are the same, but he uses the example of homosexual acts to demonstrate how far certain people had fallen away from acknowledging the truth about life and about God. He writes:

> Although they knew God they did not honor him as God or give thanks to him, but they became futile in their thinking and their senseless minds were darkened. Claiming to be wise, they became fools, and exchanged the glory of the immortal God for images resembling mortal man or birds or animals or reptiles. Therefore God gave them up in the lusts of their hearts to impurity, to the dishonoring of their bodies among themselves, because they exchanged the truth about God for a lie and worshiped and served the creature rather than the Creator, who is blessed for ever! Amen. For this reason God gave them up to dishonorable passions. Their women exchanged natural relations for unnatural, and the men likewise gave up natural relations with women and were consumed with passion for one another, men committing shameless acts with men and receiving in their own persons the due penalty for their error. (Rom 1:21–27)

Here, Paul seems simply to assume that *everyone* would know that these particular acts were clearly wrong. He doesn't even take the time to try to make a point as to *why*. Not because the *why* isn't important; it is. But likely it is because there was no dispute over the point among his readers; it was merely understood and accepted by them as part of God's truth.

Of course, this doesn't mean that Saint Paul was unfamiliar with the relatively common Greco-Roman practice of sexual relations within one's gender. In fact, he had lived in the city of Corinth in his travels and knew the reputation of people there.

This also doesn't mean that Saint Paul was insensitive to or afraid of men and women who had been practicing homosexuals. Remember, they were among his first converts in Corinth!

Saint Paul is not insensitive to people who have sexual sins in their lives! He encourages them in love and hope! But he also calls them out of those actions. This is vitally important for all Christians to acknowledge. As we have noted before, all those who follow Jesus are called to deny certain desires that do not align with God's plan and purpose.

Case of Mistaken "Identity"?

When it comes to the issue of Christians who identify as gay or lesbian, some have made the claim that Saint Paul didn't understand that homosexuality was part of the human experience, or that he didn't understand the concept of loving, committed, same-sex sexual relationships—or that maybe Paul didn't grasp the concept that one's sexual attractions were more than mere desires. Some people assert that he could not have comprehended the modern claim that one's sexual attractions comprise one's identity. On these grounds, some people hold that, Paul's prohibition of same-sex sexual acts could and should be adapted for modern times. By that they mean, in effect, that we can disregard Paul's teaching on the matter, in preference to contemporary ideas and attitudes.

There are more than a few problems with this argument. Here we note only a few. First, even if it were true that Paul didn't have the range of modern ideas about same-sex attractions at his disposal, he did have God's Word and the Holy Spirit's guidance to illuminate his teaching about human sexuality and marriage. Contemporary ideas don't alter the fundamental realities of Christian life: that human sexuality is intended to orient people toward the opposite sex and that marriage is a union of a man and a woman that is by nature oriented to the procreation of children. That human sexuality, like other dimensions of human life, is damaged by the fallenness of human existence, all of which Paul recognized, doesn't change the basic nature and purpose of human sexuality. Second, it's an unproven assumption that Paul never encountered people living in committed homosexual relationships. Indeed, from what we know about the ancient world, we can say Paul knew of such things.

As we noted above, Paul's concept of personal identity is more rooted in becoming a "new creation" in Jesus than in anything else. Even regarding his own life, Paul considers his pedigree and accomplishments a "loss because of the surpassing worth of knowing Christ Jesus my Lord" (Phil 3:8). Therefore, regardless of whether Saint Paul saw homosexual desires as innate, involuntarily acquired, or chosen, he was not concerned with an identity outside of who he (or anyone else) was in Christ. To understand God's purpose for human life, for Paul, is to understand human beings in light of their being called to become "new creations" through Christ, living according to Jesus' teaching and example.

But Jesus Never Said . . .

But what about Jesus? Wasn't he always talking about love? How could the God of the New Testament who loved *everyone* possibly have anything against *love*?

Well, there are those who argue that Jesus never said anything about homosexuality. Therefore, based on his silence, he must have had no objections. One problem with this claim is that it misrepresents what we know about Jesus and his teaching. Jesus' teaching *did* have something to say about homosexuality. As we shall see, Jesus understood sex relations to be intended for marriage, and he taught that God had designed marriage as a permanent union between a man and a woman. But even granting, for the sake of argument, that Jesus didn't do what I just said he did, those looking for an endorsement of homosexuality from Jesus are essentially arguing from silence. Such an argument isn't sufficient to show that Jesus was at odds with his Jewish religious and moral world on such a basic point. What's more, Jesus never explicitly condemned pollution or kidnapping. Does this mean that he endorsed those actions? Of course not. Following the same line of reasoning, it is not tenable to maintain that because Jesus never explicitly addressed the issue of homosexuality this tells us he would approve of same-sex activities today.

Well, what do we know about Jesus' attitude toward human sexuality and moral behavior? From the picture that Scripture presents of him, Jesus *did* have a strict sexual ethic, which was not based on some esoteric and abstract rule. Jesus knew the human heart. He understood human nature. "But Jesus did not trust himself to them, because he knew all men and needed no one to bear witness of man; for he himself knew what was in man" (Jn 2:24). It is not reasonable to claim that, if only Jesus had known the pain of loneliness or if only he had understood the way the heart longs for love, then he would surely have condoned any possible expression of that affection. Not only did Jesus know human nature, at virtually every step he was appropriately sensitive and compassionate about our wounds and our weaknesses. He understood how difficult sexual purity can be. He was tempted in every way, but, unlike us, he never sinned.

Although Jesus knew how challenging his teachings would be, he also knew that following those teachings was the key to our freedom and happiness. As a result, he was very clear in what he taught. He didn't give us a free pass on account of our weaknesses. Of course, this applies not just to Jesus' teaching about human sexuality but to all his teaching. Read what he says about forgiving our enemies (see, for example, Mt 6:12; Rom 12:14; and Eph 4:32). That's not easy but it is necessary. If we expect to be forgiven our sins, then we have to be willing to forgive others their sins.

When it comes to human sexuality, Jesus was at once understanding of our weaknesses and direct about how we should behave if we want to find the blessedness he promised. He elevated the common teaching about human sexuality, returning it to God's original purpose. For example, when questioned about divorce and remarriage, Jesus responded with the challenging teaching, "Whoever divorces his wife and marries another, commits adultery" (Mk 10:11). This teaching was met with shock. "Moses allowed a man to write a certificate of divorce" (Mk 10:4). This was part of the Mosaic Law: a man could divorce his wife and marry someone else. But Jesus insisted on the stricter standard that is part of God's original plan: "For your hardness of heart Moses allowed you to divorce your wives, but from the beginning it was not so" (Mt 19:8). Jesus, the God of love, did not hesitate to place demands on people when it came to love. He was willing to reveal clearly that love demands *more*. However, he didn't leave us alone in our weakness. Rather, he provided us with the grace to live out these teachings.

Even to a broken human heart, Jesus teaches that indulging in sexual fantasies is a serious sin. "You have heard that it was said, 'You shall not commit adultery.' But I say to you that every one who looks at a woman lustfully has already committed adultery with her in his heart" (Mt 5:27–28). Now let's make a distinction here: Jesus is not talking about simple sexual attraction or even temptations. Those are *feelings* and no one always controls his feelings at all times. But we can control what we *do* with our feelings. Jesus is talking about how we respond—acting on those feelings even if the action takes place only in our minds and hearts.

And this brings up one of the points that I have been trying to make with this book. Because we are all fallen human beings, there is no one of us who does not have *some wound* in the area of our sexuality. Whether people experience heterosexual, homosexual, or bisexual attractions, people experience at one time or another sexual feelings and attractions that aren't good for them to act upon or embrace. Someone's woundedness could manifest itself in a sexual attraction for members of the same sex, or in a desire to look at porn, or in a desire for someone who is not one's spouse, or in a desire for any number of other things. Even within marriage, spouses sometimes have to deal with feelings that can make it a challenge to respond to one another appropriately when it comes to sexuality. This is why the virtue of chastity—virtue by which we act properly with respect to our sexuality—is important for everyone. The question for each of us is not, "Am I *wrong* to have these feelings?" The question is, "What am I going to *do* with these feelings?"

Passion as Permission

Jesus clearly taught that sex belongs within in the context of marriage. He condemned fornication (see Mk 7:20–23), which is sex outside of marriage, as well as adultery and lustful actions (see Mt 5:27–28). In other words, he accepted the common sexual morality of the Old Testament. Marriage has, as one of its essential elements, the relationship between one man and one woman, as we have seen. Not only did Jesus endorse the traditional Jewish beliefs about marriage, but, as noted above, he raised the bar even higher by expressly forbidding divorce and remarriage. His teachings clearly show that he favored *fidelity* over romance! (Not that he was against romance.) And for Jesus, God intended fidelity in marriage to be the fidelity of a *man* and a *woman* to each other, which he said was God's purpose from the beginning, in making human beings male and female (see Mt 19:4–6).

Jesus' teaching that God intended marriage to be permanent (and exclusive, hence no adultery) and between a man and a woman, implies that same-sex sexual relationships are contrary to God's purpose for human sexuality. This is why it is false to talk as if Jesus' teaching has nothing to say about same-sex activity. While not everyone is called to marriage, everyone is called to the proper use of his sexuality (chastity)—people with same-sex or heterosexual attractions and feelings, married and unmarried people. That proper use of human sexuality excludes fornication—sexual activity outside of marriage—and lustful activities (sexual fantasies). People with same-sex attractions, like heterosexual people who are unmarried, are called to love people in other ways besides sexual activity. And married people are called to engage in sexual activity as God intends it, without adultery or lust.

Let's look at this topic a little more closely. I recently had a conversation with two college students, a young man and a young woman who had been dating for about a year and a half and who were hoping to get married one day. They were making a case for why the Church's teaching on sexual morality didn't apply to them. "Look," they said, "we already know that we are committed to each other, and we know that we are going to get married. Sex is one of the ways we express our love for each other. When we are together in that way, it strengthens our love for each other."

I hear a story like this at least a couple of times a month. I always try to be sensitive to these well-meaning lovers. But I have found that one of the justifications that people offer for any kind of sexual action—homosexual or heterosexual—is the fact that they are in love. This is a temptation for all human beings across the board. Unfortunately, when it comes to deep sexual feelings or romantic feelings, people will often point to their passions as some kind of implied permission to act on those feelings. That's why you have the man who says, "I can't stay married to Beth because I'm not in love with her anymore. But I *am* in love with Susan. Therefore, I *have* to act on this. To do otherwise just wouldn't be honest." Behind this thinking is the view that we are most truly what we feel, and to act against this feeling is to be less than true to ourselves. But Jesus addresses us at a deeper level than feelings; he speaks to our minds and wills as the deeper part of who we are. Of course, we can use romance to justify anything. We can use our personal sense of happiness to justify anything. But, based on Scripture, it is very clear that Jesus favors fidelity over romance. Feelings, it seems, are not enough. And given the way our feelings often go, it is good news that God does not determine who we are by what we happen to be feeling at the moment.

Looking for Loopholes

The teaching of Jesus is always liberating. But it is also often difficult. It is not surprising, given the heroic call that Christ issues, that we can be tempted to look for loopholes that can let us off the hook. For instance, some might say that Jesus was a product of his culture, so his teaching might be appropriate for his time and place, but it no longer works for ours. In a sense, it is true that Jesus was a person of his culture. But it is only a partial truth. Of course, Jesus was a Jewish man who lived in the first century, so he reflected elements of the culture of his time. But he's also the Eternal God who is unlimited by time. As God, his teachings are not culturally conditioned. Rather, he is the one who formed the Jewish culture. It is good to remember that the way of life taught by God to the Jews was in many ways countercultural even for the Jews themselves. They were constantly tempted to turn away from it and succumb to the cultural pressures around them. God was teaching the Jews, and in Jesus he was teaching the world, a universal way of love that transcended all cultures. If Jesus is the Son of God, then he cannot and must not be ignored or considered irrelevant to our time and culture. What Jesus taught about sexual union being only for marriage, and about God's plan for marriage from the beginning involving one man and one woman, applies to us. It's part of the permanent message Jesus came to teach.

Here is another common loophole some try to use: people will find ways to interpret Scripture to fit their own ideas and lifestyles. I had an interesting email correspondence with a man who had been raised Catholic. When he was twenty-seven years old, he began living an openly "gay lifestyle." In the course of our email correspondence, he addressed this challenge to me: "If you can show me where Jesus prohibited same-sex sexual relationships, I will believe it." (Apparently, Saint Paul wasn't enough for him.) In the same message he told me that he also didn't agree with the Church's teaching on divorce and remarriage. His parents had divorced and had both entered into second marriages that were significantly happier than their first. He thought the Church's teaching on this was too narrow and revealed a lack of true compassion. Since he was basing his claims that homosexual actions were legitimate on the argument from Jesus' silence about it, I posed him this question about the issue of divorce and remarriage.

"If I can show you exactly where Jesus prohibited divorce and remarriage, would you believe it then?" I asked. He agreed; so I began by showing him where Jesus strictly prohibits divorce:

> Pharisees came up to him and tested him by asking, "Is it lawful to divorce one's wife for any cause?" He answered, "Have you not read that he who made them from the beginning made them male and female, and said, 'For this reason a man shall leave his father and mother and be joined to his wife, and the two shall become one'? So they are no longer two but one. What therefore God has joined together, let no man put asunder." They said to him, "Why then did Moses command one to give a certificate of divorce, and to put her away?" He said to them, "For your hardness of heart Moses allowed you to divorce your wives, but from the beginning it was not so." (Mt 19:3–8; see also Mk 10:11–12; Lk 16:18)

In addition, Saint Paul reiterates Jesus' teaching:

> The wife should not separate from her husband (but if she does, let her remain single or else be reconciled to her husband)—and . . . the husband should not divorce his wife. (1 Cor 7:10–11)

> Thus a married woman is bound by law to her husband as long as he lives; but if her husband dies she is discharged from the law concerning the husband. Accordingly, she will be called an

adulteress if she lives with another man while her husband is alive. But if her husband dies she is free from that law, and if she marries another man she is not an adulteress. (Rom 7:2–3)

Yet, even after I showed him this very clear evidence of what Jesus *did* teach regarding divorce and remarriage, the man refused to accept it. Instead, he pointed to some biblical interpreters who claim to have found a way to dismiss Christ's teachings as "not meaning what you think they mean."

I think that this example is telling and resonates with my own experience. I know that there are times when I am facing some challenging aspect of Christ's teaching, and I want to find a loophole that lets me out of it. But when I do that, what am I really doing? With my words I am saying, "Jesus, I am willing to follow you," but with my actions I am really saying that I want to follow myself.

Picking and Choosing?

Others may argue that many of the rules in the Bible, especially the Old Testament, no longer apply. For example, the Old Testament teaches that men should not trim their sideburns and that adulterers should be executed by stoning. Yet we all agree that these laws no longer apply. This is an interesting claim, and it goes back to how we read the Bible. As Pope Benedict XVI points out in his book *Jesus of Nazareth*, there are at least two different kinds of laws in the Old Testament: apodictic laws and casuistic laws.[1]

Generally speaking, apodictic laws are those direct moral commands that are true at all times and all places for all people.

---

[1] Pope Benedict XVI, *Jesus of Nazareth: From the Baptism in the Jordan to the Transfiguration* (New York: Doubleday, 2007), 123–27.

These are instances in which God clearly states a universal moral law, like "You shall not kill," or "You shall not steal." Casuistic laws are more case-based kinds of laws. Examples might be found in the Book of Leviticus. But even here we have to be careful. For example, according to Leviticus, "Every one who curses his father or his mother shall be put to death" (20:9), or, "If a man commits adultery with the wife of his neighbor, both the adulterer and the adulteress shall be put to death" (20:10). In the case of those two laws, the severe criminal punishments for violating them are no longer in effect but the underlying commandments that makes them wrong—"Honor your father and your mother" and "You shall not commit adultery"—remain. They remain seriously sinful things that can lead to spiritual death.

Apodictic laws, by their very nature, are meant to endure beyond culture and beyond a particular time. Casuistic laws are by their very nature rooted in a particular time and in a particular culture.

Another way to look at this question is to note that there are, roughly speaking, three kinds of laws in the Old Testament: laws pertaining to the Israelite kingdom, laws concerning the Temple, and laws of morality. The kingdom laws teach how to live in the Kingdom of Israel. The Temple laws tell us how to worship and how to act in the Temple, and the moral laws are those laws regarding human moral behavior that are true at all times in all places for all people. Now why do we pay attention to the moral laws, and not the kingdom or Temple laws? The main reason is that the purposes of the Kingdom of Israel and the Temple have been fulfilled in Christ. Israel has been transformed into the Church, and the Temple sacrifice has been fulfilled in the sacrifice of Christ, now commemorated in the Mass.

Neither the original Israelite kingdom nor the Temple are now in existence in their earlier form. Therefore, the laws that pertained to them no longer apply.

Yet, the moral laws—those apodictic laws that govern human behavior and are oriented toward the good of human persons—are still in effect because human nature is a constant: we are still here.

CHAPTER TWELVE

A Real Relationship

I sat there watching the video, my ears growing warm. My younger brother had pulled up a YouTube video of a man sharing his story. In it, he recounted how much he loved his same-sex partner for a number of years. Their story ended in a great deal of pain, as his partner had died by falling off the roof of their apartment building. This tragedy was clouded in mystery and surrounded by the question of how such a seemingly avoidable accident could have happened.

It was truly sad and troubling. Also unsettling was what I gathered my brother was trying to say by asking me to watch the video. As the young man unfolded the story of how much he cared for his partner, he also revealed much of the pain they experienced in their relationship: pain not from each other, but from each other's families—more to the point, from his partner's family.

He related how his family was incredibly happy for him and would invite him and his partner over all the time. His nieces and nephews accepted them both with open arms.

His partner's family, on the other hand, had a very different and more violent response. Essentially, their reaction to the news that their son was dating a man was that "if you two ever show up on our front porch, we will meet you at the door with a shotgun." Even after their son's tragic death, they threatened this man and prohibited him from attending the funeral. They even threatened his life if he showed up.

As I watched the video, my ears grew warm because I wasn't sure how to respond. First, there was a tragic story of two men who cared about each other and loved each other. Sure, there was also the baggage of identifying as gay, which of course has a huge emotional weight to it. I love my brother, the man who was showing me this video, and it seemed like he was trying to tell me that this was a life that he wanted to pursue. Clearly, these kinds of things are emotional for everyone involved and everyone who cares. Second, and more important to me at that moment, I didn't know what was being asked of me. There are times people share stories because they touch their hearts or because they communicate something they have experienced. In those cases, one can get a powerful picture of the pain many people face in "coming out."

But there are other times when you are being shown something because you are about to be asked a question. When the video ended, my brother turned to me and asked, "So, what do you think?" At first, I wasn't sure what to say— not because I wasn't moved by the story I had just watched, and not because it caused me to question my beliefs, but because I wasn't sure what my brother was asking.

Then, in a flash, it became clear: he wanted to know *which response* I would have to *him*. In the video, there were two clear and very distinct responses. The first was from the man on the video's family: we love you and accept you. The second was from his partner's family: we are disgusted by you and reject you. This is why my ears were warm, because I was being given my two options. Either I accepted him and everything my brother chose, or I hated him.

I asked him, "Are those my only two choices?" I have asked many people this same question. Are my only two choices unqualified acceptance or hate? In my work with people of all ages, it has become clear to me that every one of us desires acceptance.

Almost all people fear rejection and desire acceptance by others. We are in various ways made for each other, and we are made to be in relationship. Therefore, it makes sense that one of the more painful things we experience on an emotional and spiritual level is rejection. One of the things that can make us feel loved and confident and most ourselves is when we know that we are accepted by the people around us.

We must be careful here. On the one hand, we don't want to say that wrong behaviors should be accepted as good or neutral, even when society generally thinks such behaviors are good or neutral. Whether something is good or neutral isn't determined by a vote or a popular poll. On the other hand, we must be careful that in our rejection of wrong behaviors, we don't reject people, especially people who may already be marginalized.

I think of a young woman named Emily. She was raised Catholic and truly loved Jesus and the Church. She was very involved in our youth activities and is an incredibly funny and talented young woman. When Emily was in her junior year of high school, she came out as a lesbian. Her family continued to love her (and even celebrated her homosexuality); the response of the local church was focused on making sure that she knew that she shouldn't act on her attractions. To be fair, this is one important role of the Church. In fact, it is one of the works of mercy, an expression of love, to teach people how to live in such a way they can grow in friendship with God, have the most joyful life they can have in this world, and come to everlasting happiness in the next. But, looking back, I think that Emily could have benefitted from a better pastoral approach.

Like so many young people who experience same-sex attractions, Emily had already been battling a certain degree of shame and self-condemnation about her sexuality. Even though she hadn't acted on her same-sex attractions at that point, her view of herself was that she was too different from the other kids at church. She saw herself as someone who *needed* to hide this deep and important part of herself.

When she "came out," she wasn't rejected by her youth ministers or priests. On the contrary, they made plenty of room for her and continue to communicate with her regularly. One of the problems was, whenever they shared the Church's teachings on this topic with her, she interpreted their words and actions as pushing her away. This highlights one of the dilemmas we face as we confront this issue with both truth and love.

You Don't Want to Push Anyone Away!

Abortion. Divorce. Same-sex attractions. These are some of my favorite things to preach on. I have to tell you, I just can't wait to get up in a pulpit and try to sum up the Church's teachings on these volatile topics in fifteen minutes or less. It's just so much fun and brings me so much joy. When I see people squirm, just knowing that I might be inadvertently making them uncomfortable (or better yet, hurting them emotionally), I just experience so much happiness.

Of course, I'm being sarcastic. While I delight in preaching the truth of Jesus, it is a challenge to speak into these contested issues. That's why, when I have to say something about these difficult topics, I strive to be as conscious as I can regarding who might be on the receiving end of my comments. No matter how gentle or sensitive I've tried to be, someone will invariably approach me after Mass or after a talk and say something like, "Father, you shouldn't talk about these controversial issues. After all, you don't want to push anyone away."

I often want to grab this person and ask, "Did you hear what I said? I clearly said that people who have had an abortion have a God who can forgive them and restore their hearts. I clearly said that God knows all about your broken marriage and broken heart and can heal you. I thought that I was explicit about how every same-sex attracted person has a home in the Church."

I don't know how many times I have been misunderstood when I've preached on these topics. No doubt part of the problem is me. I'm not perfect at communicating on sensitive issues, and I blame myself for my shortcomings. But there seems to be more going on. In any case, when I address sensitive topics, there is almost always someone who misunderstands what I am trying to say.

There could be any number of reasons for this misunderstanding. For example, sensitive topics demand a balance between charity and truth. Such topics are often profoundly complex, and the right wording is difficult to find. In addition, in our culture today we often understand certain words differently. A priest or minister might use a term in its properly understood theological context, but others perceive a different meaning.

But it seems to me that the main reason there is so often misunderstanding (and why talking about these topics can feel like pushing people away) is a problem of interpretation.

This is not to diminish the actual rejection or unjust discrimination that many people face. Such occasions are all too real. What I am talking about are those situations where rejection is a matter of misperception.

Interpretation

There is first the action, and then there is our interpretation of the action. People have their own motivations for their actions, and they usually know the reason they choose to do something. And that's something we should acknowledge—although people can sometimes be self-deceived in their motivations.

But that is not the only element at play. We also have our own interpretation of the action, an interpretation that will be informed by our history. I am sure everyone who has been raised in a family can understand the situation of a seemingly innocuous comment from one family member to another. If you were an outsider walking in, you would've thought, "Oh well, whatever." But this seemingly innocuous comment might be interpreted as meaning something more insulting or more unkind in the light of past experiences.

Our worldviews are shaped by our life experiences and our interpretations of things that happened to us. As a kid, I had what would kindly be called a big gap-toothed grin. My teeth were all over the place. But I never even gave it a second thought. Why not? Looking back, I think that I didn't have any hang-ups about my smile because I had been regularly affirmed in that exact area. I can remember people coming up to me and telling me how much they liked my smile. Consequently, I didn't think that there was a problem because of the compliments I had received. The goofy part of my smile didn't even register for me. Now, other parts of my body I have been weirdly self-conscious about. Some concerns are based on *one thing* that *one person* said at *one time*. This one comment, for whatever reason, has colored how I perceive myself in those areas.

This happens in relationships as well. We can see this on a daily basis. When you are in a relationship where you know that the other person or people love and respect you, it is relatively simple to interpret their actions through that lens. Say a friend made a last-minute change of plans to go out with you. If you know you are loved and respected by your friend, you are more likely to interpret the change of plans in the best possible light. You will assume that there must be a good reason for the cancellation. Or if you knew that your friend was occasionally irresponsible you might chalk it up to failing to follow through. But you probably wouldn't regard it as a personal rejection.

With all of this in mind, it becomes clearer why many people who experience same-sex attractions are sensitive to anything that even *seems like* rejection. Other people should be appropriately aware of how their words and actions could be misinterpreted as rejection. It's not that any particular group needs to be coddled; it's because same-sex attracted persons often have experienced shame and rejection— whether as a result of their own sense of their sexual woundedness, or from overt or subtle actions by others. In either case, the result is often that people have been pushed to the margins.

For people used to assuming others would reject them "if they only knew," the wound of rejection greatly affects how they interpret the words and actions of others. For those without this particular experience, it can be helpful to remember similar things in their lives that affect how they interpret other people's words and actions.

Let's Have a Real Relationship

A young man named Danny recently shared with me a part of his experience of being same-sex attracted and Catholic. Danny was raised in the Church. Not only was his family actively involved in his local parish, but Danny attended all the retreats, camps, and other youth group events that were offered. He became a leader among his peers.

Around the time that Danny entered his freshman year of high school, he became more and more aware that he was attracted to men. This was heartbreaking for him because he wanted to be a good Catholic and his same-sex attractions were torturous to his young heart. Three things happened in Danny's life that were absolutely critical.

First, the summer before his freshman year of high school, he went on a weeklong retreat designed to help teenagers learn how to pray. That week was transformative. Prayer—real conversation with God—became the center of Danny's spiritual life. In his own words, Danny said, "When I felt like I couldn't turn to people in the Church, and when I myself didn't like who I was and what I was feeling, I could turn to God in prayer, and he was able to remind me that I was still good. That I was still his son."

The second thing that happened was that Danny realized his same-sex attractions were not a "phase." He wasn't mistaken about it. At first, this awareness was an incredible burden. He returned again and again to prayer, pleading, "God, please take this away. Don't make me feel this way." But coming to the place where he acknowledged that these desires were persistent and not merely transitory helped lead to the third thing that happened.

This third critical movement in Danny's life involved acceptance. Father Romano Guardini is a noted master of the spiritual life. He was one of the giants of the Christian faith of the last century. In a book on the virtues, Father Guardini comments on the virtue of acceptance. Not many people consider acceptance to be a virtue in the strict sense. But Guardini points out that it is among the first (and most necessary) of all the virtues. In response to the question, "What do I have to have in order to grow in the moral life?" he writes: "I believe, we would have to answer, 'It is the acceptance of what is, the acceptance of reality, your own and that of the people around you and of the time in which you live.'"[1] Guardini is not talking about weak submissiveness or passivity. He reveals what true acceptance involves. First, he writes, one must accept oneself.

> For I am not a man in general, but this particular person. I have a certain character and no other, a certain temperament among all of the various ones that exist, certain strong and weak points, definite possibilities and limitations. All of this I should accept and build upon as the fundamental basis of my life.[2]

If we fail to do this, we can't progress in the spiritual life. I do not necessarily have the same strengths or the same struggles as another person. I can find myself rebelling against my struggles or dismissing my strengths, but if I want truly to grow as *myself*, then I must accept reality. That is to say, I have to accept myself as I actually am, not as I would like to

---

[1] Romano Guardini, *Learning the Virtues That Lead You to God* (Manchester: Sophia Institute Press, 1998), 25–26.
[2] Ibid., 27.

be. I must acknowledge my limitations, my weaknesses, and my strengths.

This is the opposite of approving of everything and leaving everything unchanged. The kind of acceptance Guardini is speaking about makes possible the transformation we so desire. I can and should work on myself and my life and mold and improve it. First, however, I must admit the existing facts; otherwise, everything becomes false.

There are two sides to this act of acceptance, of facing reality. The first and most important is to accept my fundamental identity as a child of God, made for love, capable by God's grace of reaching perfection and fulfillment. This is the ground of all spiritual growth. The second act of acceptance is to be honest and clear about my current state: how I am put together, what experiences I have had that have influenced me, how the wound that every fallen human being experiences is working in my life. If I don't make the first act of acceptance concerning my true identity in Christ, I will get lost in the confusion of identities swirling around me. If I don't make the second act of acceptance concerning my current state, I will not be facing reality, and my relationship with God will be founded on an illusion.

For Guardini, acceptance is not the same thing as resignation. Resignation is often the endpoint. It is the place where I stop. If I am resigned to my fate, I may be giving myself permission to cease moving forward. But when I am willing to accept myself and my circumstances, I can truly begin.

In his book *Hatchet*, Robert Paulsen tells the tale of a thirteen-year-old boy named Brian Robeson whose plane crashes in the North Canadian wilderness. There is a critical moment in the story when Brian realizes where he is, how far he is from home, and what he must do to survive. This realization crushes him, and he begins to sob. As Paulsen writes,

> When he sat alone in the darkness and cried and was done, all done with it, nothing had changed. His leg still hurt, it was still dark, he was still alone and the self-pity had accomplished nothing. He did not know how long it took, but later he looked back on this time of crying in the corner of the dark cave and thought of it as when he learned the most important rule of survival, which was that feeling sorry for yourself didn't work. It wasn't just that it was wrong to do, or that it was considered incorrect. It was more than that—it didn't work.[3]

Brian accepted his situation. Fighting against reality doesn't work. Denying one's situation doesn't help. At the same time, Brian was not resigned to his fate. Resignation means, "I now have permission to stop moving, to stop trying." Acceptance means, "I acknowledge and accept who I am and where I am. With that knowledge and acceptance, I am prepared to move forward."

Guardini writes,

> Of course, we can change and improve many things and shape them more according to our wishes, especially if these wishes are definite and the hand that seeks to carry them out is firm. Basically, the tendencies that have grown out of our earliest years remain and determine what follows. Psychologists say that the fundamental characteristics of a child are fixed by the end of his third or fourth year. These accompany him through his later life, as also do those influences which the persons around him, the social group, the city, and the country have exercised.[4]

---

[3] Gary Paulsen, *Hatchet* (New York: Simon and Schuster, 1987), 79.

[4] Guardini, *Learning the Virtues*, 29.

Finally, Guardini points out that we have to accept our destiny. As we said earlier, destiny is not the same thing as fate. Fate is something that is fixed. It goes against the notion that we have free will. But to have a destiny implies that one has a destination. To have a destination means that a person has purpose. There is a place beyond this place that a person was made for. It is this destiny that we can choose to live for. Consider the boy in *Hatchet* who had to accept himself, his situation, and the fact that he had somewhere to go. Acceptance of his destiny is what moved him out of his self-pity and hopelessness and started him on the path home.

Danny's moment of acceptance came when he was in Adoration as a junior in high school. He had been praying that God would take away his same-sex attractions. But then, as he looked at Jesus in the Blessed Sacrament, something moved within him. In that moment, he said to the Lord, "God, this is me. I know that you accept *me* and love *me*."

These three moves were life-changing for Danny. Without his devotion to prayer, and without a genuine acceptance of himself, his circumstances, and his destiny, he wouldn't have been able to move forward as a same-sex attracted man and as a Catholic. He is also moving forward as *celibate*. Danny's knowing that God accepts and loves him is not the same thing as thinking that would God condone all of his actions. Danny decided to accept God's call to express love in a way different from sexual activity.

This is the kind of acceptance that all of us are called to embrace. Regardless of our situation in life, and regardless of the strengths and weaknesses each of us experience, we must accept the truth about ourselves—both our high destiny and our current wounds—and move forward. Acceptance of these realities is the precondition for being transformed, changed ever more truly into the image of God. This is what it is to have a real relationship with God. If I do not let God find me and love me as I currently am, I will never allow God to find me and love me, because God always deals with realities, not illusions. I must always accept the truth of what I am, in order to be open to the possibilities of what God can help me become.

When my brother showed me the video of the same-sex attracted man who lost his partner, I think he was looking for acceptance—not from himself but from me; he was looking to see if I would deal with him as he is. And I fully accept and embrace my brother. I accept the fact that he identifies as gay. When I embrace him, I'm embracing a man who understands himself as gay. But of course, this is not the same thing as agreeing with every decision that he makes. In the same way, he can love me and not agree with every decision I make because we have a *real* relationship.

As my dad said when my brother came out, "No good parent accepts every one of his children's decisions." He added, "Some parents do, but no *good* parent does."

CHAPTER THIRTEEN

Questions and Answers

Common sense has become so rare it should be classified as a superpower.

—Anonymous

In the course of my ministry, I am often asked by parents to talk about what they should do after their son or daughter has announced that he is gay or she is lesbian.

Unfortunately, sometimes parents distance themselves from a same-sex attracted son or daughter or family member who identifies as gay. Sometimes families even kick a child out of the house. Even worse, some families say, "Well, we are Christians. This is a Christian family. You don't belong here." This is the opposite of the message of Christ.

The message of Christ, and the message of the Catholic Church is: You do belong here. This is your family. We will never kick you out.

Now, people sometimes leave, but we will never kick them out. Sometimes people walk away, but we will never kick them out. Sometimes people run away, but we will never kick them out. They can always come home. This is the message.

Sometimes families raise questions with commonsense answers, but because the questions involve issues of same-sex attractions, common sense goes out the window. Families can mistakenly think these issues are special cases in which common sense doesn't apply.

Not so; common sense does apply. It doesn't mean the rules go out the window. It doesn't mean we should say, "Oh, because you identify as gay, our family's rules no longer apply to you." It doesn't mean we should say, "Oh, in this case I can't ask you to respect the wishes of our family." It goes both ways. In families and in the Church, we must respect our same-sex attracted brothers and sisters. And it is also reasonable to expect our brothers and sisters to respect us.

With that commonsense principle as background, we turn to some common questions.

Question: My son wants to bring his boyfriend home for Christmas. What do I do?

I remember hearing someone ask Father John Harvey, the founder of Courage,[1] this question years ago. He answered, "Well, invite them both!" What he was getting at is that, since the person in your son's life is obviously important to your son, a special occasion like Christmas provides an opportunity to show respect and get to know him.[2] Many families open their homes to friends and neighbors during special occasions, including the holidays.

Father Harvey was concerned, though—as many parents would be—that parents in this situation do not give their

---

[1] Courage is an apostolate of the Roman Catholic Church for men and women who experience same-sex attractions. Founded by Fr. John Harvey at the request of Terence Cardinal Cooke, Courage invites men and women with same-sex attractions to live lives of authentic love and friendship as disciples of Jesus Christ in the Catholic Church. Find them online at www.couragerc.org.

[2] Cf. Fr. John F. Harvey, OSFS, and Gerard V. Bradley, *Same-Sex Attraction: A Parent's Guide* (South Bend: St Augustine's Press, 2003), 202–3.

children mixed messages. We've talked a lot about how a same-sex relationship is not part of God's plan for sexuality, and so neither the Church nor individual Christians can celebrate when two people of the same sex are living and acting as a romantic couple. This is not just an opinion that you as parents happen to believe. It's an important part of the faith that shapes your life, and that you are responsible for sharing with your children.

Some people who identify as gay or lesbian experience profound isolation and feel distant even from the people who should love them the most. The last thing parents want to do is to make a son or daughter feel unwelcome. Your son or daughter should always be welcome in your home, and on special occasions, it can be important to welcome their partner, too.

At the same time, giving a real welcome means more than being kind and friendly; it also means speaking the truth with love, even when that truth is, "I love you very much, but I think you're making bad decisions." The faith that is at the center of your family is not just something to think about: it requires a response. We respond to faith by living a moral life, by embracing God's plan and striving to follow it. So, if a son or daughter brings a partner home for a special occasion that involves an overnight stay, you should be clear that they will be staying in separate rooms.

Consistency is needed here, or else your son or daughter will feel singled out. My own family had this covered: When a family member came out as gay and wanted to bring his boyfriend home, it was a straightforward situation for my parents to handle, because they already had clear expectations for all the other members of the family. When siblings, cousins, or nephews and nieces came to visit, it was always the same rule: "Okay, if you have your significant other, that's wonderful. You are sleeping in different rooms." As parents, this should be the expectation for all your unmarried children, whether their significant other is of the opposite sex or the same sex.

Question: My daughter came home from her first semester at college and told us that she identifies as a lesbian. What do I do?

Here are my suggestions. First, *don't panic.* Your daughter has revealed something very personal about her life, and it probably took a lot of courage for her to open up to you. Stay calm, affirm her for trusting you with this important part of her life, and assure her that your love for her isn't going to change.

Second, and this is very important, *listen to her.* Listen to what she says; listen to her experiences. As Pope Francis has said, "In life, God accompanies persons, and we must accompany them, starting from their situation."[3] When you let your daughter take her time to tell her story, both you and she can begin to understand more clearly where she's coming from and what she's looking for.

It's natural that you will be concerned about what you hear, and that this news will shake what you thought your daughter's life was like and how you thought her future would unfold. But I suggest you resist the temptation to give a lecture, or to correct the way she's thinking right away. Try to avoid what may come across to her as an interrogation—"Wait. Are you *sure*? How do you know?"—and take time to listen and understand it from her perspective.

The third thing I suggest is that you don't try to "fix" her. Many parents, upon learning their child is experiencing

---

[3] Antonio Spadaro, SJ, "A Big Heart Open to God: An Interview with Pope Francis," *America*, September 30, 2013, https://www.americamagazine.org/faith/2013/09/30/big-heart-open-god-interview-pope-francis.

same-sex attractions, ask, "What do I do now? How do I get it so that my child doesn't feel this way anymore?" *It is not your responsibility to "fix" your child.* It's also not very productive, at least at this point, to focus on questions like, "Where is this coming from? Why did this happen? Is it my fault?"

Next, I recommend that you affirm everything that you can affirm without compromising your faith. Your daughter may say something like this: "I am a lesbian and I have this incredible friend. We are dating now, and she just gets me. She's so easy to talk to; she's so funny. She constantly builds me up, and we help each other."

If you can see that there are the foundations of a real friendship there, acknowledge them! Friendship is a different kind of love from sexual love, of course, and by letting your daughter talk about her relationship, you can help her to see the difference. Same-sex intimacy is always wrong, and so romantic feelings that are leading toward a sexual relationship aren't appropriate in a real friendship—in fact, they make friendship much harder to achieve. When real friendship can take root, though, it can be a real help in living a moral life. As the United States Conference of Catholic Bishops has written, "True friendships are not opposed to chastity; nor does chastity inhibit friendship. In fact, the virtues of friendship and of chastity are ordered to each other."[4]

Finally, look for an opportunity to speak from the perspective of faith about God's love for your daughter and his plan for her life. Your first conversation may not be the right time for a full-blown catechism lesson about sexuality

---

[4]   United States Conference of Catholic Bishops, *Ministry to Persons with a Homosexual Inclination: Guidelines for Pastoral Care* (Washington, D.C., 2016), 11.

and chastity. That part of the conversation can come later. But it can be very important to reassure your daughter, not only that she hasn't lost your love, but that she is and always will be a beloved daughter of God the Father. Let her know that your concerns for her decisions and for her future come from your conviction that God created her with a purpose; that God has a plan for her body and her soul, for her sexuality and her relationships; and that ultimately happiness and holiness are the same thing, that following God's plan for our lives leads us to true fulfillment. Let her know that you will always be praying for her to know God's love and embrace God's plan more fully.

Of course, you daughter may try to get your blessing for her relationship. This is understandable. At the same time, you should not think affirming as much as you can means you must agree with everything she thinks is good in her relationship or agreeing with all of her choices. You may need to find language to express that you understand how she feels about her relationship, that you love her no matter what, and that you hope she understands that loving her doesn't mean agreeing with everything she chooses to do or everything she thinks, any more than her loving you means she must agree with everything you choose to do or you think.

Question: I keep blaming myself for my son being gay. Did I do something wrong with how I raised him?

When we are upset, it is common to look for something or someone to blame: "Why did this happen?" "How did this come about?" We look for somewhere to place our focus so that we can fix something. But this situation is not one parents are in a position to "fix."

It's also understandable that parents may look to themselves to try to understand what they see as a problem with their children. But, in this case, that's not going to be very helpful.

We don't know the origin of same-sex attractions. Some people theorize a genetic basis for them. Others think it's a developmental issue. Others associate them with traumatic childhood experiences. A few people describe same-sex attractions as a matter of choice, but most same-sex attracted people don't say they chose it. Of course, whatever the explanation, it doesn't follow that same-sex attractions should be acted on, any more than it follows that other attractions or inclinations we may have should be acted on, just because we did not choose to have them.

Many men and women who experience same-sex attractions say they don't recall a time when they *didn't* feel this way or at least didn't feel different. Others associate their attraction with some experience. Perhaps they got really close to a member of the same sex, and then that closeness, that intimacy, became sexualized. I also know of individuals who entered into same-sex relationships as a result of abuse, but that is a different kind of story. There might be some events or attitudes that could contribute to a person being sexually attracted to members of the same sex. But as a parent you don't need to weigh all the theories and hypotheses about the origin of your child's feelings. Your task at this moment is to love God and to love your child.

Question: Our son recently told us that he is gay. We love him and want to remind him that he is welcome home, but we are concerned that his younger siblings could get confused.

First, it is good that you are clear about loving your son and letting him know that he is welcome and that he is part of the family.

Second, you are rightly concerned for *all* your children. Your other children may be vulnerable to confusion. Some or all of them may not be sufficiently mature to respond appropriately to your son's same-sex attractions. They may not be able to make certain distinctions. (Things like, "We love your brother, but don't agree with all of his choices.") They may be misled into challenging the Church's teaching about sexuality and marriage. They may not be prepared to know how to respond in love to their brother. So be wise about what you say and how you say it.

Depending on your relationship with your son, you may ask him how he thinks the matter should be handled. He probably has some sense of how his siblings see things or are likely to do so. This also could really help address the issue of feelings of isolation or rejection. It can be helpful to include him in your decision-making process—if you think he can see the bigger picture of the family situation and he won't respond based only on what he regards as his best interest.

He also needs to be able to respect your role as parents and not to take offense if, after hearing his perspective, you decide you must act differently from what he desires. On the one hand, you aren't leaving the matter wholly to your son's determination—you are the parents, after all, and you have primary responsibility for your other children. On the other hand, by talking with your son, you are trying to include him in the process. You can communicate that he is still part of the family. If he is involved, even if the decision is to keep this from some of the younger siblings for a while, what might have been experienced as a moment of rejection can instead be a time of inclusion.

Question: My daughter keeps saying that we can't really love her unless we accept and embrace her as a lesbian.

Your daughter regards her same-sex attractions as a critical element of her self-identity. For her, it is not as if she just dyed her hair pink or she wants to dress a certain way. She sees her homosexual feelings as an important part of who she is. Therefore, she tends to think your acceptance of her lesbianism is tantamount to your acceptance of her as a person.

Nevertheless, you can accept that your daughter is same-sex attracted and that she regards her attraction as an important part of her identity. Loving her doesn't require approving of everything she thinks or does, any more than her loving you requires that she approves of everything you think or do, as I have repeatedly noted elsewhere in this book.

I once spoke with a woman named Susan whose younger brother, Jack, has a homosexual orientation. Susan, who honestly couldn't have cared less one way or another about her younger brother's sexual orientation, gave him this piece of wisdom. She said, "The sooner you come to accept that Mom and Dad are not going to change their beliefs about homosexual actions, the happier you are going to be in the long run." At first Jack was a bit shocked, and he responded, "But if they love me, then they need to change their beliefs and accept me." To her everlasting credit, Susan remained the loving voice of reason and she said, "Jack, in the first place, you are asking Mom and Dad to accept you, but you don't seem willing to accept them or their beliefs. And in second place, if you don't want them to try and change you, then you ought not to try to change them."

At that moment, Susan reminded Jack that he was being challenged to accept his parents with their core beliefs as Christians, just as they were being challenged to accept him with his core experience of same-sex attractions.

Your daughter wants a relationship with you, and you want a relationship with her. But good, healthy relationships always have boundaries. You can have a real relationship with your daughter and be able to disagree with her. You can expect her to love you and accept you in the same way that she is asking for your love and acceptance. I do not believe that this is too much to ask. It is a sign that you love each other as *equals*. That is the key. Loving each other as equals means that we can disagree and still love each other.

Question: Do I need to speak out every time the topic of same-sex attractions comes up?

It depends on what you mean by "speak out." Certainly, you should always show by your life the witness of your faith. That's a kind of "speaking out." But that witness can take on different forms in different situations.

For example, often the Church is presented as narrow-minded and constantly obsessed with keeping people from doing things they want to do. The Church is presented as simply saying no all the time. When it comes to same-sex attractions, the Church doesn't just say no. The Church says same-sex attracted people have dignity and can live holy lives. She says that they are capable of living chastely, of directing their sexuality to the service of God and living a fulfilled Christian life, as everyone is called to do, including unmarried people. She says they can and must love others, including in nonerotic ways.

What's more we can also "speak out" in not treating everything about same-sex relationships as bad or seeing only what we regard as wrong with such relationships. We can affirm the positive without endorsing everything about the relationship or leaving the impression we approve of what we regard as contrary to the teaching of Jesus and God's plan for human sexuality.

That said, there may be times when our "speaking out" must be vocal and it must be challenging. If people generally experience us as loving, accepting people, who are willing the good of others and who are willing to see good where it exists, even if it also includes things we regard as evils or problems, they will be more inclined to listen to what we have to say that can be taken as critical.

Question: What if I am invited to my child's same-sex wedding?

More and more Christians will find themselves facing this dilemma as our culture continues to move toward widespread normalizing of same-sex relationships.

Here's my view of the matter. What does "going to a wedding" mean? What does your presence at a wedding "say"? We know that those at the wedding are, in a sense, *witnesses*. There are, of course, the legal witnesses in the wedding party. But all the guests serve as witnesses to the oath the couple is making. You never merely watch a wedding; you witness a wedding. One's presence at a wedding usually implies a form of approval and endorsement of what is happening.

This means, of course, that there are many weddings that a Catholic cannot attend in good conscience. A second marriage when a person's first spouse is still living (unless the Church has established that the first wedding ceremony did not create a permanent bond); a wedding involving a Catholic that takes place before a justice of the peace, or in someone's backyard, or on the beach, without special permission; or a civil wedding between two people of the same sex, are all invalid from the perspective of the Catholic Church's teaching and law. We can't take part in these wedding ceremonies, no matter how closely we may be connected to the bride or groom.

This might sound harsh or difficult. But in reality, while it might be difficult, it is not harsh. It is simply the consequence of being a disciple of Jesus. Jesus says that if we're in a situation in which a father or mother, brother or sister, threaten to come between him and us, we must choose him if we want to be his disciples (Lk 14:26; cf. Mt 10:37). If I am not willing to make this choice, then I am not willing to be a Christian when it makes a difference.

There is such a thing as scandal. To scandalize, in the Christian sense, does not mean simply "to shock"; it means that acting in such a way as, in effect, to call something wrong "right" or vice versa. In this way, we wind up encouraging others to do something wrong by our bad example.

As I said earlier, people who expect us to "accept" them in love, even though they make choices we regard as wrong, can't reasonably expect that they shouldn't have to accept us, when we make choices they regard as wrong. As Christians, we can ask for the same respect as others expect of us. We might be tempted to think, "If I love my child, I have to go to his wedding to show him that I love him." I can understand why someone might think that way. But in fact, simply because your child thinks what he is doing is right doesn't mean he has the right to force you to do something against your conscience or to act publicly in a way you think will mislead others, as a condition of your loving him.

There is no doubt that what I am saying can be difficult. It can be a challenge to find ways to communicate that you still love your child, even if you can't, in good conscience, attend his same-sex wedding. You should ask the Lord for the strength and the love to remain steadfast to him and to help your son know that you still love him.

Question: I have been asked to be the godfather of my nephew. My brother and his partner are my nephew's adoptive parents. What should I do?

The United States Conference of Catholic Bishops wrote that "Baptism of children in the care of same-sex couples presents a serious pastoral concern. Nevertheless, the Church does not refuse the Sacrament of Baptism to these children, but there must be a well-founded hope that the children will be brought up in the Catholic religion."[5] This raises an important point about Baptism: that it is not just about the ceremony, but has an impact on the entire life of the person who receives it.

Sometimes the Church asks a pastor to delay the celebration of Baptism, if there is a concern that the parent(s) of the child will not be able or willing to raise the child in the faith and bring him to the other sacraments. When the people who have adopted the child are living as a couple in a romantic and sexual relationship, they are publicly acting in a way that is the opposite of an important teaching of the faith, on the morality of sexual intimacy. Because they are public about their relationship, it is not just appropriate but necessary for their parish priest to talk with them about it. If they are unwilling to consider the call of the Church to embrace chastity, it is hard to see how they will be able to teach the faith to their child, since they are not fully living it themselves.

When they are open to striving to live in accord with what the Church teaches, then this helps the priest to have a well-founded hope that they will share this teaching with the child. This is also the place where the role of the godparent comes in. A godparent, also known as a sponsor, takes on the responsibility of helping the parents to impart the faith to the child, and to live that faith more fully themselves. If you take on the role of godparent for your nephew, you are also making a commitment to your brother and his partner to hold them accountable for living as good Christians, and to help them to understand and embrace God's will for their lives.

---

5   Ibid, 21.

CHAPTER FOURTEEN

The Ultimate Question

Throughout this book I have written about the experiences of people who identify as gay and lesbian. Yet I have not privileged their accounts of their experiences at the expense of Catholic teaching. I am saddened by what seems to be an attitude of exceptionalism among some same-sex attracted Catholics—the idea that they are exceptions to Catholic teaching. In other words, "The Church's teachings don't apply to me because..."

The reasons that some people who identify as gay or lesbian give for why Church teaching supposedly doesn't apply to them run the gamut. "Because I have always felt this way." "Because heterosexual couples fail to live up to the Church's standards." "Because feeling this way isn't my fault." "Because the Church hasn't listened to the experiences of gay and lesbian Catholics." "Because the hierarchy doesn't know what it is to live with my experience." "Because there is no such thing as 'pray the gay away.'" "Because I just want someone to know and love me."

"God, I know what you want. But I want what I want." If that's your outlook, then I want formally to welcome you to the human experience. People with same-sex attractions aren't unique in their struggling to do God's will. We are all called to say yes to God in how we live our lives. We all experience in various ways the temptation to say no and to act on our will against God's will. Often we see ourselves as exceptions, when in reality we aren't. The temptation toward exceptionalism is not restricted to Catholics who identify as gay and lesbian. We are *all* tempted to make exceptions for ourselves. We are all tempted to say, "I know what the Lord asks, but *in my case* things are different." We are all in the same boat, even if our experience of the boat is somewhat different. That is why I constantly have to reiterate when I am speaking to groups about the Church's teaching in this area that this is not about us and them; this is all about us. This is about "we." And we are all called to be saints.

As Christians, we must be closer friends with Jesus than we are with the world. This means our lives must say yes to Jesus, before anything else. As a result, I may find myself having to say no to some things so that I can say yes to Jesus, my first friendship above all others. Again, this applies to everyone, those with heterosexual attractions and those with homosexual attractions.

All of this comes down to one question: Do I trust?

Like Eve in the Garden, I am tempted to distrust that obeying God will lead to *more* in life than disobeying (cf. Gen 3:1–6).

Like the Lost Son, I am tempted to distrust that the Father still loves me and that I have a place in his family (cf. Lk 15:11–32).

Like Sister Melanie, I am tempted to distrust that God knows my true origin, story, and destiny.

Like anyone who is just tired of fighting, I am tempted to wonder if all of this is really worth it.

Like anyone who is lonely, I am tempted to distrust that I will know the heights and depths of love by following the path given to me by Jesus.

Jesus shows you and me the way:

Like Jesus in the Garden, I want to trust the Father even in the face of death (cf. Mt 26:36–46).

Like Jesus on the Cross, I want to trust the Father's silence and commend my spirit into his hands (cf. Mt 27:45–50).

Like Jesus with his genealogy and difficult origin, I want to trust that the Father knows my true origin, story, and destiny.

Like Jesus in the desert, I want to persevere with purpose (cf. Mt 4:1–11).

God has a plan for your life. God has a vision of the lives of all of those whom you love. Trust him with it.